EXCERPTING AMERICAN HISTORY
FROM 1492 TO 1877

EXCERPTING AMERICAN HISTORY FROM 1492 TO 1877

Primary Sources and Commentary

First Edition

Written and edited by
J. Edward Lee, Ph.D.

Winthrop University

cognella®
SAN DIEGO

Bassim Hamadeh, CEO and Publisher
Peaches diPierro, Developmental Editor
Alisa Munoz, Project Editor
Jeanine Rees, Production Editor
Jess Estrella, Senior Graphic Designer
Greg Isales, Licensing Coordinator
Natalie Piccotti, Director of Marketing
Kassie Graves, Vice President of Editorial
Jamie Giganti, Director of Academic Publishing

3970 Sorrento Valley Blvd., Ste. 500, San Diego, CA 92121

For my students: past, present, and future.

Brief Contents

Detailed Contents

Acknowledgments

First, allow me to thank the excellent professionals at Cognella Publishing for approaching me in October 2020 about this project. When they floated the idea, I grabbed hold, and we steered toward our shared goal of producing a readable and affordable survey of American history. Thanks, team members, Susana Christie, Alisa Muñoz, and Peaches diPierro.

As always, I appreciate the enthusiastic support of my wife, Ann-Franklin Hardy Lee; daughter Elizabeth Lee Walen; son-in-law Corey Walen; and grandchildren Madeline and Connor. Just as the first Americans brought their families, my own family has always accompanied me on my journeys through our nation's past.

My forbearers arrived in Virginia in 1640. The first was Richard Lee, "the immigrant," and his wife, Ann Constable. We are all, in a sense, immigrants; many of our forebears stepped ashore under "duress," and I acknowledge their courage and sacrifice. Their DNA is powerful, and I get tremendous satisfaction trying to tell their stories.

Finally, I never forget my students. Since I walked to the university lectern for the initial time in 1985, they have inspired me with a hunger for answers to the age-old question, "Who are we as a people?" Throughout my 36-year career in the university classroom, I have attempted to suggest answers to that question.

J. Edward Lee, PhD
York, South Carolina

Introduction

Studying history allows us to walk backward through time, seeing the people and events of the past with a new understanding of their lives and times. While it is impossible to come physically across the land bridge, Beringia, connecting Asia and North America, we can ponder the trek that those first Americans took 30,000 years BCE. They left no written record of their journey, but by considering the factors that motivated these people, we gain an appreciation of their journey across the glacier before it melted. Similarly, a walk backward allows us to grasp the collision of cultures caused by Christopher Columbus's arrival on the beaches of the Caribbean in 1492. Why did things turn out as they did?

On our walk, we ask ourselves important questions: "Why did Great Britain's American colonies declare their independence in 1776?" "Who were the ringleaders of such an event?" "Could this 'divorce' have been prevented?" "Why did the Founding Fathers succeed?" "Who did they exclude from their belief that 'all men are created equal'?" "Why does change take so long?" It is questions like these, the collection of historical evidence and the interpretation of this evidence, that makes our walk into America's past so invaluable.

This anthology begins with the journey across frozen Beringia. Along the way, we meet men and women who we have heard of before: Thomas Jefferson, Abigail Adams, and Benjamin Franklin, for example. But many people we encounter remain nameless actors, such as the Bostonians who helped toss East Indian Tea into the harbor on a December night in 1773. Or the women who argued at Seneca Falls, New York, in 1848 for gender equality. Who were they? What did they want? Or the slaves who received word on January 1, 1863, that President Abraham Lincoln had emancipated them. What does freedom mean to people who have never tasted it? Can we better understand fundamental questions about gender, race, conflict, and economic empowerment? In history, we ask important questions that, in a sense, help us understand ourselves.

Our walk backward begins with commentary entitled "These United States: Themes Emerge." Underlying themes shape our past, such as cultural interaction, the growth of the American Empire, freedom, and violent arguments over human bondage. These themes are evident in the primary sources of our past—documents that educate us about who we have been and how we have treated each other over the centuries.

These United States: Themes Emerge

Early in my career, a prominent mentor, Dr. George Brown Tindall of the University of North Carolina at Chapel Hill, advised me, "Always teach the United States History Surveys." Dr. Tindall, in fact, had just published his own textbook for use in those survey courses, essential curricular foundations of all history departments. For 36 years, I have followed Dr. Tindall's advice. While I teach upper-level and graduate history courses, too, at Winthrop University, where I am the director of graduate studies, the surveys, divided at 1877 in history departments across America because that milestone is when Reconstruction ended, are invaluable to all students, offering them a basic knowledge of our people and the themes of American history.

In this anthology, we commence with the arrival in the Caribbean in 1492 of Christopher Columbus; proceeding to the collision of cultures; advancing to competition between European nations; sliding into the American Revolution; drafting the United States Constitution for posterity; forming a new republic; shoving indigenous people aside; sweeping forward across the continent during Manifest Destiny; being poisoned by the brutality of slavery, which became an addiction; experiencing the devastation of our Civil War; and concluding with the failure of Reconstruction to successfully reconstruct the Union. The first half of the United States survey, 1492 through 1877, is the story of nearly four centuries of America's search for its identity, a story of heroism, hardship, justice, cruelty, and learning to coexist with different cultures.

The themes of American history shout out to us: a restless, rebellious, inquisitive people encountering other ethnicities, clashing with one another, flirting with worthy ideals, experiencing sectional differences and tensions, slowly marching for justice and inclusiveness, growing and moving westward, and quarreling over basic human rights. We, after all, are a young nation. We should remember that fact. Even in the twenty-first century, we see remnants of these early themes in our culture. What, exactly, is the basis of our republic? It is a question still being pondered today.

Primary sources, I stress to my students, are the raw material of history: the letters, speeches, fundamental government documents, diaries, journals, newspapers, and manuscripts that allow us to form judgments about our past. For this anthology, I have selected 50 of these primary sources with introductory essays prepared by myself, followed by questions to be considered. "Thinking Historically," I call these questions. Ponder them and search for answers to them in the multitude of sources available to today's university students. Cognella's talented mapmakers prepared five maps to illustrate the themes of growth and tension. Maps show us important geographical landmarks, which clarify the movement of populations such as ours.

It should be emphasized that this survey is designed to be student-friendly, using excerpts of history's raw materials, which coalesce to provide us with a clearly written tour through our past. We take slivers of our past and let the words speak to us. Before we begin with the consideration of people who arrived on this continent under duress thousands of years before Christopher Columbus, let us examine three of these primary sources.

Document 0.1. The Declaration of Independence of 1776

The American Revolution did not commence on July 4, 1776. Tensions between the mother country and its 13 American colonies had been building for a century. Trade regulations, called Navigation Acts, benefited Great Britain. No colonist sat in Parliament; there was no actual representation in that lawmaking body—only virtual representation. Revenue-raising acts became onerous after Great Britain's costly victory in the French and Indian War. King George became increasingly unpopular in Britain's colonies. The "official" Anglican Church received privileges at the expense of other religions. British troops quartered themselves in colonial homes and patrolled the streets of cities such as Boston, ensuring that the colonists were obedient to the mother country. Thus, Congress meeting in Philadelphia in the early summer of 1776 boldly appointed a committee to draft a Declaration of Independence. Virginia's Thomas Jefferson, a slave owner and gifted writer, prepared the document, targeting the monarch; it is excerpted here:

> When in the Course of human events, it becomes necessary for one people to dissolve the political bands which have connected them with another, and to assume among the powers of the earth, the separate and equal station to which the Laws of Nature and of Nature's God entitle them, a decent respect to the opinions of mankind requires that they should declare the causes which impel them to the separation. We hold these truths to be self-evident, that they are endowed by their Creator with certain unalienable Rights, that among these are Life, Liberty, and the pursuit of Happiness. That to secure these rights, Governments are instituted among Men, deriving their just powers from the consent of the governed. That whenever any Form of Government becomes destructive to these ends it is the Right of the People to alter or abolish it, and to institute new Government, laying its foundation on such principles and organizing its powers in such form, as to them shall seem most likely to effect their Safety and Happiness.

Thinking Historically

1. What audiences was Thomas Jefferson trying to influence with the Declaration of Independence?
2. What did "all men are created equal" mean in 1776? Now?
3. Why did Jefferson target King George and not Parliament for the grievances?
4. Why has this document had such a lasting effect on our nation and the world?
5. Are there still lessons to learn from the Declaration?

Document 0.2. The Women's Declaration of Sentiments

Change moves slowly, and we see that clearly in the movement for gender equality. Thomas Jefferson and the other Founding Fathers omitted women from positions of power in the first century of our nation's history. In 1848, however, we had fulfilled our goal to conquer North America, sweeping across the continent all the way to the Pacific Ocean. The war with Mexico, triggered by a questionable military clash between the Nueces and Rio Grande Rivers and by America's dreams of Manifest Destiny, resulted in the acquisition of an empire that stretched from the southwest to California. Sensing that the time might be right to voice their goal of women's rights, Elizabeth Cady Stanton and Lucretia Mott called for a meeting in Seneca Falls, New York, to promote this goal. The excerpted Women's Declaration of Sentiments, which blamed the male gender for promoting inequality, spells out the women's argument.

> When, in the course of human events, it becomes necessary for one portion of the family of man to assume among the people of the earth a position different from that which they have hitherto occupied, but one to which the laws of nature and of nature's God entitle them, a decent respect to the opinions of mankind requires that they should declare the causes that impel them to such a course.
>
> We hold these truths to be self-evident: that all men and women are created equal; that they are endowed by their Creator with certain inalienable rights; that among these are life, liberty, and the pursuit of happiness; that to secure these rights governments are instituted, deriving their just powers from the consent of the governed. Whenever any form of government becomes destructive of these ends, it is the right of those who suffer from it to refuse allegiance to it, and to insist upon the institution of a new government, laying its foundation on such principles, and organizing its powers in such form, as to them shall seem most likely to effect their safety and happiness.

Thinking Historically

1. Why did the women of Seneca Falls believe the timing was right for their appeal?
2. Why did they target the male sex for their grievances?
3. Why did their Declaration not produce the change that the women considered long overdue?
4. What lessons should we learn from the failure of the Declaration to achieve this change?
5. Why did women not receive equality until the next century?

Document 0.3. The Emancipation Proclamation

By 1863, our nation had been fighting its bloody Civil War for two long years and thousands of northerners and southerners had lost their lives. Union President Abraham Lincoln had initially explained the conflict's purpose as preserving the Union, restoring the southern states to the Union, and ensuring that the slaveholding border states did not secede. By 1863, however, Lincoln boldly changed his justification for the war: it was now about ending slavery, the system of cruel human bondage that had led to the South's secession beginning in 1860 with South Carolina's exit and the formation a few months later of the Confederate States of America. Excerpted next is Lincoln's Emancipation Proclamation, which did not apply to the border states and boldly recast the war in moral terms.

> That on the 1st day of January, A.D. 1863, all persons held as slaves within any State or designated part of a State the people whereof shall then be in rebellion against the United States shall be then, thenceforward, and forever free; and the executive government of the United States, including the military and naval authority thereof, will recognize and maintain the freedom of such persons and will do no act or acts to repress such persons, or any of them, in any efforts they make for their actual freedom.

Thinking Historically

1. Why did President Lincoln change his mind in 1863 about the purpose of the Civil War?
2. Was he trying to send a message to European nations, as well as the citizens of the North and the South?
3. Why did he exclude the border states, where slavery existed, from his proclamation?
4. How did slaves react to Lincoln's proclamation?
5. Why did the leadership of the Confederate States initially not take the proclamation seriously?

As this thematic introduction makes clear, our survey of America deals with significant issues, such as human rights, gender, and ethnicity. Each chapter will provide an essay written by the author, sprinkled with excerpts from significant primary source documents like the three in this introduction, and supplemented by appropriate maps. The "Thinking Historically" questions are designed to generate thought, discussion with peers, and further research. Students of the twenty-first century are wizards at exploring the Internet and can identify a treasure trove of information on these important themes and documents. Ask significant questions as we start our journey: "Who, exactly, are we?" "Why have we moved in various directions?" "What factors have motivated us?" Additionally, you will be able to ponder the historian's craft and what I call the 5 Ws of history: "Who?" "What?" "When?" "Where?" "Why significant?" We begin our survey with consideration of prehistory and the arrival of the first Americans, people who came here under duress.

DURESS

Historians form partnerships with scholars from other disciplines as they tell the story of the past. In recent years, we have seen the fields of political science, sociology, psychology, economics, and geography provide invaluable research that historians can use. After all, history studies people, their motivations, their interactions with one another, their environment, their conflicts, and their organizations. Libraries, archives, and electronic repositories supply the modern historian with written, visual, and recorded primary sources. In prehistory, however, the people are long gone, and they left no written materials about their lives. We would err if we viewed the arrival of Spanish explorer Christopher Columbus in 1492 as the beginning of America. He did, in a sense, "open" the door to the New World, and it remained open, but people were here long before Columbus's 1492 Caribbean encounter with indigenous Americans. That is why historians enlist the expertise of archaeologists, researchers who sift through the artifacts and relics of vanished civilizations, and scientists who study climate to understand an era stretching back 30,000 years. Those early inhabitants, while not having a written culture, have important things to tell us about our past. Their voices cannot be heard, and their diaries cannot be read, but these first Americans speak to us through the remnants of their movements during prehistoric times.

Squinting through the haze of history, we can imagine groups of humans searching for food making their way fearlessly across the 1,000-mile-wide land bridge called Beringia, still frozen by glaciers, from Asia to North America 30,000 years Before the Common Era (BCE). One of the themes of American history is movement, a restlessness. These first Americans, nameless but breathing and walking, brought their families to a new land in search of big game: wooly mammoths and bison. Archaeologists, those scholarly cousins of historians, have discovered projectile points used for the hunt, inserted by hungry and restless people into the ribs of these ancient beasts, yielding food and fur to protect the immigrants from harsh weather.

Americans arrived thousands of years ago under duress, hungry, desperate, restless dreamers seeking new opportunities in the land across Beringia. It would be descendants of these first Americans who would stand curiously on the Caribbean beach in October 1492 to greet Christopher Columbus and his sailors, many themselves under duress, glory-seeking wanderers searching for economic gain. The story of America commences with pressured individuals, wanderers and hunters, and risk takers. The Old World and the New World became, in a sense, connected. A "Columbian exchange" between Columbus and the natives was about to begin. Food, animals, crops, and knowledge would be part of this exchange, but it ultimately would be tragic for the Native Americans who fell victim to smallpox and cruelty at the hands of whites.

Earlier archaeologists tell us humans had migrated into Asia from Africa. We are descended from these migrants, evolving over eons, who moved from Africa to Asia and, finally, 30,000 years BCE, crossed Beringia's expanding glaciers in a quest for mammoths weighing as much as nine tons each, giant sloths, bison, ox, and caribou. Scarcity of food motivated those prehistoric people, and the New World offered them an abundance of natural resources.

These early Americans were strangers in a strange land, they and their families. As the glaciers melted, some arrived in small boats from Pacific islands, making their way into America where, eventually, they would meander southward and construct pueblos and burial mounds. The history of America starts with faceless individuals huddled around campfires, slowly filtering into the darkness of a continent full of potential and new challenges for humans under duress. A canopy of green awaited them, under which there was nourishment. Feeding upon shellfish, kelp, and pink salmon, these people were in an American Garden of Eden, brimming with food such as sheep, birds, enormous panthers and tigers, and deer. Domesticated wolves assisted the human hunters and gatherers. Tools, pottery, hooks, baskets, bones, pots, jewelry, primitive weapons, and artwork have been unearthed by archaeologists, created and used by anonymous immigrants who learned to survive and thrive in America. History's artifacts, dug from ancient dirt by archaeologists, document the lives of men and women who came across that land bridge connecting Asia and North America 30,000 years ago. They would be followed in 1000 AD by intrepid Norsemen (Vikings) from Scandinavia, masters of the sea with their painted vessels, fearlessly crossing the Atlantic Ocean nearly 500 years before Columbus, landing at Vinland and Newfoundland, near the present border between Canada and the United States, surveying the terrain, camping but returning to their European homeland.

It would be the first Americans, those who made their way across Beringia, who stayed. They migrated southward into Central and South America. They constructed intricate civilizations: the Mayans, the Aztecs, and the Incans. Eventually, these civilizations would encounter European explorers who would take from them their land, wealth, lives—wrecking their civilizations. These first Americans, whose ancestors brought their families and dreams across the frozen terrain thousands of years earlier, arrived under duress, seeking food for empty stomachs and seeing a New World with unlimited potential. They would be the indigenous people who witnessed the events of the autumn of 1492 when Columbus sailed into view. He, unlike the Norsemen of five centuries earlier, had no intention of returning to the Old World empty-handed. As the Columbian exchange, a cultural collision, commenced, neither world would ever be the same.

Document 1.1. Map of Beringia

This map illustrates the migration of the first Americans, 30,000 BCE. A frozen land bridge, 1,000 miles wide, connected Asia and North America, enabling migration to occur

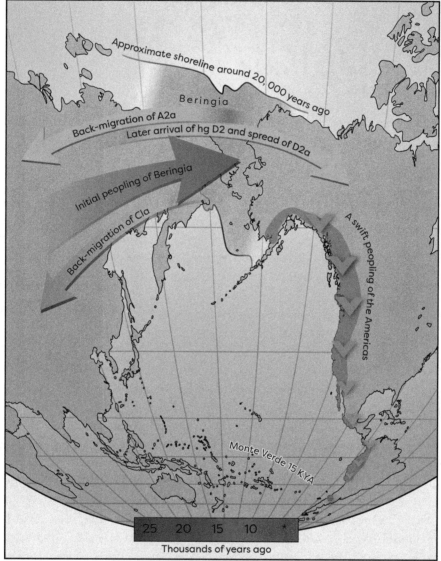

Thinking Historically

1. Discuss the importance of the search for food as a motivation for the first Americans.
2. Did the melting of the glaciers strand these people in America?
3. Why did they proceed further into the continent?
4. Does the lack of a written record hamper our understanding of them?
5. Why did the Norsemen not remain in the New World?

COLLISION

O ne of the themes of our nation's history is ethnic interaction. Sometimes, these "exchanges" are positive and invigorating. Unfortunately, they can also be violent and debilitating, draining an ethnic group of its identity and vitality. As we consider the collision of cultures that occurred with Christopher Columbus's arrival in what he mistakenly thought to be the Orient in 1492, we are struck by the fact that perhaps 100 million Native Americans occupied what we consider "the New World." As we have seen, these first Americans crossed Beringia before the glaciers connecting Asia and North America melted, thousands of years prior to 1492. Tragically, their number would, through disease and genocide, number less than a million by the twentieth century. This ultimate destruction would not be evident in 1492, however, as Columbus set foot on the Caribbean beach.

Born in 1451 in the Republic of Genoa, Columbus was enamored with the sea from a young age. His father was a weaver of wool, and he became a dream weaver. Hearing exploits of older sailors, Columbus yearned for glory and riches. The wealth of China had been glimpsed by Marco Polo two centuries earlier, and a land route, the Silk Road, had been traveled by entrepreneurs. This trek was full of danger; it was perilous and populated by bandits. Could a water route be quicker and safer?

From 1482 to 1492, Columbus and his brother Bartholomew had lobbied European monarchs to finance a western voyage to the spices and silk of the East Indies. After initially being rejected by Spain's King Ferdinand and Queen Isabella, the Spaniards in 1492 agreed to sponsor Columbus's dream because they had successfully united their domain, repulsing Muslims southward into North Africa. The monarchs proclaimed him an admiral with authority over "all those islands and mainland in the Ocean Sea which by his hand and industry he would discover and acquire."

In August, Columbus and three shiploads of adventurers headed west into the Atlantic Ocean. Some of his crew became disillusioned and whispered of mutiny as time passed with no land in sight. But Columbus, in his early 40s and hungry for recognition and wealth, sailed forward. On October 12, 1492, land was sighted, but one of history's greatest miscalculations had occurred. The approaching land was not the East Indies. Unknown to the admiral and his band of followers was the fact that they had stumbled on the islands of the Caribbean. The indigenous people standing on the beaches were not "Indians." This misnomer has remained. These "Indians," in Columbus's judgment, initially were "noble savages" who could lead him to wealth, cities of gold, and acclaim. He intended to convert them to Roman Catholicism. Soon, sadly, these first Americans would be regarded as "savages."

Christopher Columbus tried three more times to reach his goal of Asian markets by water, but Central America stood in his way. There was a collision of cultures underway, and there would be no retreat like that which occurred four centuries earlier with the Norsemen. This Columbian exchange between Europeans and Native Americans was extensive: food, language, livestock, crops, and disease. Spain's other explorers, like Hernando de Soto and Ponce de León, would compete with the Portuguese, such as Vasco de Gama and Ferdinand Magellan.

Two years after Columbus's historic first voyage, Pope Alexander Borgia signed the Line of Demarcation, which divided this New World between Spain and Portugal. Other Europeans ignored this edict: Henry Hudson probed Canada for England. The French arrived, also, in Canada, with Jacques Cartier searching for the nonexistent Northwest Passage to the Orient. Jesuit priests searched for Catholic converts. The Netherlands sent explorers to New Amsterdam (New York). Permanent cities arose: Quebec for France, Saint Augustine for the Spaniards. And, in 1585, Queen Elizabeth of England authorized a settlement along the outer banks of present-day North Carolina at Roanoke, which would be known as the Lost Colony. Three years later, when Spain and England waged war with each other, this British colony disappeared.

Great Britain redoubled its efforts in Jamestown, Virginia, in 1607, where ill-prepared colonists a few years later endured the Starving Time with cannibalism. Further ethnic interaction occurred in Jamestown in 1619 when tobacco planter John Rolfe noted in his journal, "Today, 20 or so (Africans) arrived." There would be no cities of gold in America, but the animals, crops, and lumber were invaluable. Tobacco was popular in Europe, but it is a labor-intensive crop, meaning that hard work is necessary for cultivation. If Native Americans were unwilling to perform this task, the settlers of Virginia would turn to Africans, who over the next few generations became slaves, a cruel system of human bondage that spread well beyond Jamestown. By then, the men and women who had greeted Columbus on the Caribbean's beaches in the autumn of 1492 and watched the collision of cultures had lost control of the riches of the New World.

Document 2.1. Columbus's Initial View

As previously noted, Columbus received sponsorship from Spain's monarchs to sail westward in search of the wealth of the Orient. He recorded his findings and impressions of his encounter with "Indians" in his journal. Initially, he believed they would lead him to valuable gold and serve as willing converts to Catholicism.

I saw but one very young girl, all the rest being very young men, none of them being over thirty years of age; their forms being very well proportioned; their bodies graceful and their features handsome: their hair is as coarse as the hair of a horse's tail and cut short; they wear their hair over their eye brows except a little behind which they wear long, and which they never cut: some of them paint themselves black, and they are of the color of the Canary islanders, neither black nor white, and some paint themselves white, and some red, and some with whatever they find, and some paint their faces, and some the whole body, and some their eyes only, and some their noses only. They do not carry arms and have no knowledge of them, for when I showed them our swords they took them by the edge, and through ignorance, cut themselves. ... They must be good servants and very intelligent, because I see that they repeat very quickly what I told them, and it is my conviction that they would easily become Christians, for they seem not (to) have any sect.

Thinking Historically

1. Why does Columbus provide such a detailed description of the use of paint?
2. What does his mention of weapons tell us about future ethnic interaction?
3. Why does his journal mention potential religious converts?
4. Does he clearly consider them to play a subservient role?
5. What do you think the Native Americans thought of the admiral and his crew?

Document 2.2. Columbus's 1493 Report

The admiral, who had spent ten years lobbying for support of his voyage, wished to promote a positive view of his efforts to the people back home. In the following excerpt, Columbus writes a member of the royal court in Spain about his impressions of the natives. This letter was written by Columbus in early 1493 as he headed back to Europe.

As I know you will have pleasure from the great victory which our Lord hath given me in my voyage, I write you this, by which you shall know that in thirty-three days I passed over the Indies with the fleet which the most illustrious King and Queen, our Lords, gave me; where I found very many islands peopled with inhabitants beyond number. And, of them all, I have taken possession for their Highnesses, with proclamation and the royal standard displayed ... there are many havens on the sea-coast, incomparable with any others that I know in Christendom, and plenty of rivers so good and great that it is a marvel.

Thinking Historically

1. By eagerly claiming land for Spain, what future problems was Columbus creating with the indigenous natives?

2. Does he realize yet the blunder he has made about his geographic location?
3. How will the admiral use his journal and correspondence to garner support for future voyages?
4. Is he trying to whet the appetite of Spain's monarchs for an American empire?
5. Ponder how future explorers will view the New World's inhabitants.

Document 2.3. Hernando Cortés's 1519 Impression

While Columbus tries four times unsuccessfully to reach the Indies, other explorers probed the New World too. Spain's Hernando Cortés encountered the Aztecs in present-day Mexico in 1519. He was fascinated by the natives but considered them less than human, as the following excerpt shows.

> One very horrible and abominable custom they have which should certainly be punished and which we have seen in no other part, and that is that whenever they wish to beg anything of their idols, in order that their petition may find more acceptance, they take large numbers of boys and girls and even of grown men and tear out their hearts and bowels while still alive, burning them in the presence of those idols, and offering the smoke of such burning as a pleasant sacrifice. Some of us have actually seen this done and they say it is the most terrible and frightful thing that they have ever seen.

Thinking Historically

1. Is Cortés using the human sacrifices of the Aztecs as justification for his own inhumane treatment of these peoples?
2. How did the natives become viewed as cruel "savages" within three decades of Columbus's arrival in America?
3. How should we living in the twenty-first century understand the prevalence of human sacrifice in 1519?
4. Why were the early explorers repulsed by what they witnessed in Mexico?
5. Did the lure of wealth, territory, converts, and power generate the cruelty of the explorers themselves?

Document 2.4. Chief Powhatan and Jamestown

Protestant Great Britain took Richard Hakluyt's advice a year later and set sail for the New World. Its efforts at Roanoke along the outer banks were mysterious: the settlement became the Lost Colony, disappearing around 1588 while England and Spain struggled for dominance on the world stage. Then, a colony, Jamestown, began in 1607. As the white and native cultures collided, Chief Powhatan tried to use his skills with the hungry and ill-prepared newcomers, addressing the colony's military leader, Captain John Smith.

> Think you I am so simple not to know it is better to eat good meet, lie well, and sleep quietly with my women and children, laugh, and be merry with you, have copper, hatchets, or what I want being your friend; than to be forced to flee from all, to lie cold in the woods, feed upon acorns, roots and such trash, and be hunted by you that I can neither rest, eat nor sleep, but my tired men must watch, and if a twig but break, there comes Captain John Smith: then must I flee I know not wither, and thus with miserable fear end my miserable life, leaving my pleasures to such youths as you, which through your rash unadvisedness, may quickly as miserably end, for want of that you never know how to find?'

Thinking Historically

1. What, exactly, was Chief Powhatan proposing to Captain John Smith?
2. Was the chief searching for allies among the colonists at Jamestown?
3. How extensive was division among the various Native Americans?
4. Did this division allow Great Britain and other European nations to strengthen their New World presence?
5. Why did the English fail to accept Powhatan's offer?

As stated earlier, Jamestown almost collapsed a few years later during the Starving Time, when hard-pressed colonists ate "dogs, cats, rats, and mice," supplemented by cadavers and each other. Perhaps they should have accepted a partnership with Powhatan, but they recovered when additional colonists appeared at Jamestown. Additionally, as previously mentioned, the soil could grow tobacco with the hard labor of enslaved people. Spain's power was declining after its failed fight with Great Britain in 1588. England and France were surging. But Native Americans, the indigenous people, were swiftly being pushed aside in the land where they had arrived first by competitors from a faraway place.

3

COMPETITION

After Christopher Columbus landed in the Caribbean and encountered the indigenous population, Pope Alexander VI, spiritual father of the Roman Catholic Church, divided the New World between Spain and Portugal in 1494. For the next century, a scramble occurred among European nations to claim land and to assert dominance in America. Cities like Spain's Saint Augustine (1537), England's Jamestown (1607), France's Quebec (1608), and Holland's New Amsterdam (1624) were established as permanent settlements. Further South, Portugal advanced into Brazil. The riches of the New World were not gold, but they came in the form of golden opportunities in a natural paradise flush with lumber, fertile soil, and wildlife. Explorers claimed territory for their European mother countries, missionaries claimed converts among the natives, and competition occurred, excluding concern for the interests of the original inhabitants.

Many colonists arrived for religious freedom. Dissenters like Pilgrims, fleeing Great Britain's intertwining of religion and politics, set foot in Plymouth in 1620, drafting the Mayflower Compact, a document espousing principles such as majority rule and protecting the common good. The English formed an early legislature, a House of Burgesses, at Jamestown a year earlier, the same year that John Rolfe witnessed the arrival of the first Africans. Puritans came to Massachusetts Bay in 1630, proclaiming a doctrine of hard work as the means of salvation. Any Puritan who dared to disagree with this harsh theology would be banished, as Reverend Roger Williams and "Good Wife" Ann Hutchinson soon discovered. Competition and in-fighting among Massachusetts's Puritans split the colony and ignited the 1692 Salem witch hysteria in which 19 Puritan women and one male were executed.

Maryland was founded by Roman Catholics from Great Britain in the 1630s who were loyal to King James as a safe haven. These settlers ultimately tolerated other Christians. In 1682, Quakers led by William Penn began "the Holy Experiment," a colony based on complete freedom of religion. Thus, religion motivated people of many faiths to set sail for America. Economics motivated other colonists.

In 1670, English immigrants from Barbados created Charles Town along the Carolina coast, bringing with them enslaved Africans to toil in the rice paddies of the Low Country. Rice, like the tobacco of Virginia, was a labor-intensive crop, requiring hard work by people in bondage. Once again, we see the theme of individuals under duress in the settlement of America. Slave rebellions, like the 1739 Stono Rebellion near Charles Town, illustrate the power of dreams of freedom. If they could only reach Spanish Florida, they would be free. But slave vessels continued to cross the Atlantic Ocean from Africa to bring their human cargo to port cities like Charles Town and, in the mid-1700s, Georgia's Savannah, carrying individuals who were not indentured servants working for a prescribed period of time but rather a permanent labor force enriching a class of southern planters through the sweat of their brows.

From 1739 to 1750, traveling evangelists Jonathan Edwards and George Whitefield led the Great Awakening throughout England's colonies, attracting crowds who heard sermons about salvation and lingered to discuss politics. Friction with the mother country was evident because Parliament passed Navigation Acts beginning in the 1660s. These laws benefited Great Britain by milking the colonies of their natural wealth, regulating the colonial economy. Colonists were treated like children, receiving no actual representation in Parliament. Prescribed, enumerated goods were shipped on English ships, and troops closely monitored an economic system designed to raise money for the mother country.

Competition between Great Britain and France focused on the luscious Ohio River Valley with both European countries wrestling with each other for control. Many Native Americans favored France because that nation treated them fairer. Realizing that war with France was imminent, England called upon its "children" in 1754 to prepare. The colonists, angry that Parliament excluded them from decision-making, were slow to assist their mother country. The 1754 to 1763 French and Indian War (Seven Years' War) resulted ultimately in an English victory but at considerable economic cost. Parliament would be faced with the task of disciplining its undependable American children.

Document 3.1. The 1620 Mayflower Compact

Among the English colonists were religious dissenters who wished to worship in the New World without the interference of the Anglican Church, the mother country's official and privileged church. Arriving in Plymouth, Massachusetts, in 1620, these settlers drafted an agreement designed to protect their freedom and unity. This proclamation is a powerful statement of principles that, over the centuries, have made their way into our political system.

> We whose names are underwritten, the loyal subjects of our dread sovereign lord, King James, by the Grace of God, of Great Britain, France, and Ireland King, Defender, of the Faith, etc., and honor of our King and country, a voyage to plant the first colony in the northern parts of

Virginia, do by these presents solemnly and mutually, in the presence of God and one another, covenant and combine ourselves together into a civil body politic, for our better offering and preservation and furtherance of the ends aforesaid; and by virtue hereof to enact, constitute, and frame such just and equal laws, ordinances, acts, constitutions, and offices, from time to time, as shall be thought most meet and convenient for the general good of the colony, unto which we promise all due submission and obedience.

Thinking Historically

1. Did the Pilgrims believe their geographic distance from the monarch, Parliament, and the Church of England would provide a degree of independence?
2. What, exactly, does "the general good of the colony" mean?
3. Does this agreement extend to Native Americans?
4. Is it possible that the mother country was relieved that the Pilgrims had left Europe?
5. Why did the Pilgrims sign this compact before setting foot on what they believed to be "the northern parts of Virginia"?

Document 3.2. "The Holy Experiment" of Pennsylvania

The Pilgrims were not the only religious group to venture to the New World. The Quakers, under the leadership of William Penn, also saw an opportunity to practice their faith away from the Crown and the Anglican Church when they came to America in 1682. Like the Pilgrims, Puritans, and Roman Catholics, the Quakers were trying to escape the discrimination of the mother country. The following impressions are by Quaker Richard Townsend.

> At our arrival in Pennsylvania we found it a wilderness. The chief inhabitants were Indians, and some Swedes, who received us in a friendly manner. And though there was a great number of us, the good hand of Providence was seen in a particular manner, in that provisions were found for us, by the Swedes and Indians, at very reasonable rates, as well as brought from diverse other parts that were inhabited before.
>
> Our first concern was to keep up and maintain our religious worship; and in order thereunto, we had several meetings in the houses of the inhabitants; and one boarded meeting-house was set up, where the city was to be, near Delaware. And, as we had nothing but love and good will in our hearts, one to another, we had very comfortable meetings from time to time; and after our meeting was over, we assisted each other in building little houses, for our shelter.

Thinking Historically

1. Describe the foundation of this colony's emphasis on fellowship.
2. What advantages did "the Holy Experiment" have that the Pilgrims lacked?
3. Why was the New World fertile ground for religious groups such as the Quakers?
4. What is the Quakers' relationship like with Native Americans?
5. Why will Pennsylvania's openness and fellowship aid the colony's development?

Document 3.3. The Case of Anne Hutchinson

A large group of religious dissenters arrived in Massachusetts Bay in 1630. These Puritans, at odds with the Anglican Church and the government of Great Britain, sought to build "a godly shining city on the hill." They wished to demonstrate the power of hard work, frequent religious services, and a blend of theocracy and politics. They were intolerant of dissent, expelling one of their own, Reverend Roger Williams, in 1634 to Rhode Island because he lacked Puritan fervor. In 1637, Anne Hutchison was tried for questioning the road to salvation and conducting meetings with other Puritan women in which they discussed salvation through God's grace. In the excerpt, she remains unbowed before Governor John Winthrop. Her fate would be the same as that of Reverend Williams.

> (Gov. Winthrop): Mrs. Hutchinson, you are called here as one of those who have troubled the peace of the commonwealth and the churches here; you are known to be a woman that hath had a great share in the promoting and divulging of those opinions that are causes of this trouble,
>
> (Anne Hutchinson): What have I said or done?
>
> (Winthrop): Why do you keep such a meeting at your house as you do every week upon a set day?
>
> (Hutchinson): It is lawful for me to do so, as it is all your practices; and can you find a warrant for yourself and condemn me for the same thing?
>
> (Deputy Governor): Now it appears by this woman's meeting that Mrs. Hutchinson hath so forestalled the minds of many by their resort to her meeting that now she hath a potent party in the country. Now if all these things have endangered us as from that foundation, and if she in particular has disparaged all our ministers in the land that they have preached a covenant of works, ...
>
> (Hutchinson): Now if you do condemn me for speaking what in my conscience I know to be truth, I must commit myself unto the Lord.

Thinking Historically

1. Why did the leaders of Massachusetts consider Anne Hutchinson to be a threat?
2. Comment on the role played by gender in her case.
3. What does this lack of diversity tell us about Massachusetts's theocracy?
4. What response did the authorities expect from Mrs. Hutchinson?
5. Do you see the seeds for the 1692 witch hysteria being planted in this case?

Document 3.4. The Stono Rebellion

Labor-intensive crops such as tobacco and rice encouraged white colonists to search for a solution, first among the wary natives, then indentured servants who worked for perhaps seven years before becoming free, and, finally, African slaves. Fears of slave rebellions worried planters, and in 1739, they erupted along South Carolina's Stono River, near Charles Town. Slavery had come to that colony early, and the system of human bondage distorted South Carolina, leading in 1712 to the establishment of North Carolina, with its small farms and less dependence on slave labor. Watching was the slave colony of Georgia, founded by convicts who occupied land along the way to freedom in Spanish Florida. This excerpt is from that southern colony's records. Thirty whites and 44 Blacks lost their lives in this rebellion.

> On the 9th day of September last being Sunday which is the day the Planters allow them to work for themselves, Some Angola Negroes assembled, to the number of Twenty: and one of them called Jemmy was their Captain, they surprised a Warehouse belonging to Mr. Hutcheson at a place called (Stono); they there killed Mr. Robert Bathurst, and Mr. Gibbes, plundered the House and took a pretty many small Arms and powder, which were there for Sale. Next they plundered and burnt Mr. Godfrey's house, and killed him, his Daughter, and Son. They then turned back and marched Southward along Pons Pons, which is the road through Georgia to (Saint) Augustine, they passed Mr. Wallace's Tavern towards daybreak and said that they would not hurt him, for he was a good Man and kind to his Slaves, but they broke open and plundered Mr. Lemy's House, and killed him, his wife and Child. They marched on toward Mr. Rose's resolving to kill him; but he was saved by a Negro, who having hid him went out and pacified the others. Several Negroes joined them, they calling out for Liberty, marched on with Colours displayed, and two Drums beating, pursuing all the white people they met with, and killing Man Woman and Child when they could come up to them.

Thinking Historically

1. When South Carolina's lieutenant governor, William Bull, encountered the slaves, why did he vow to make an example of them?
2. How did the dependence on slavery distort southern colonies like South Carolina?
3. Was there no substitute for the harvesting of labor-intensive crops other than slaves?
4. What does the Stono Rebellion tell us about the tensions in colonial America?
5. How do you imagine a free colony such as Pennsylvania viewed this insurrection?

Document 3.5. Reverend Edwards and the 1741 Great Awakening

Tensions between the mother country and her American children had been festering since Parliament began passing Navigation Acts in the 1660s. The colonies lacked actual representation in Parliament, restricted to only virtual representation. Smuggling was discouraged by intrusive search warrants known as "writs of assistance." British troops kept a watchful eye on the disobedient children. Additionally, the Stono Rebellion alarmed the southern colonies because it illustrated the slaves' thirst for freedom. So, beginning in 1739, a religious revival known as the Great Awakening swept the colonies. Anxious colonists gathered to hear the warnings of Reverend Jonathan Edwards (a 1741 sermon excerpted next) and his fellow minister, George Whitfield.

> Your wickedness makes you as it were heavy as lead, and to tend downwards with great weight and pressure toward hell, and, if God should let you go, you would immediately sink, and swiftly descend and plunge into the bottomless gulf; and your healthy constitution, and your own care and prudence, and best contrivance, and all your righteousness, would have no more influence to uphold you and keep you out of hell, than a spider's web would have to stop a falling rock. Were it not that so is the sovereign pleasure of God, the earth would not bear you one moment; for you are a burded to it; the creation groans with you; the creation is made subject to the bondage of your corruption, not willingly.

Thinking Historically

1. Why are Edwards and Whitefield considered Old Testament–style evangelists?
2. Why are the colonists ready to hear the harsh sermons of the Great Awakening?
3. Who, exactly, is to blame for this dire warning?
4. As the preaching ceased, what other issues did the colonists discuss among themselves?
5. What seeds are being sown for the future by the Great Awakening?

Document 3.6. Gottlieb Mittleberger, Eyewitness to Suffering

By 1750, thousands of German immigrants flowed across the Atlantic to the New World. Under duress back home, these colonists risked their lives in a six-week voyage to Pennsylvania. One German pastor, Gottlieb Mittleberger, was appalled by "the sale of human beings" in which many people died during the trip, others became seriously ill, and others were destined for indentured servitude, a system of bondage in which the individual worked seven years to pay off the cost of his or her ticket to America. The following is an excerpt from Gottlieb's journal.

> Many sigh and cry: 'Oh, that I were at home again, and if I had to lie in my pigsty!' Or they say: 'Oh God, if I only had a piece of good bread, or a good drop of fresh water!' Many people whimper, sigh, and cry piteously for their homes; most of them get homesick. Many hundred people necessarily die and perish in such misery, and must be cast into the sea, which drives their relatives, or those who persuaded them to undertake the journey, to such despair that it is almost impossible to pacify and console them.

Thinking Historically

1. What motivated the Germans to migrate to Pennsylvania?
2. How did the system of indentured servitude differ from slavery?
3. Describe the risks that colonists might encounter on their voyage.
4. How did these individuals interact with those colonists who had come earlier?
5. What conclusions can we draw about the dominance of an agricultural economy in 1750?

Document 3.7. The War with France

The 1754 to 1763 French and Indian War (Seven Years' War) ended in victory for Great Britain, but it came at a high cost. Colonists were slow to rally to the mother country's aid, and England resented this failure. The riches of the Ohio River Valley were acquired, and Britain triumphed over France in the New World, but the debt and administration of an expanded North American Empire would strain the mother country's economy and her relationship with her colonies. The struggle with France was chronicled in an 1884 mutlivolume study by historian Francis Parkman, excerpted next.

> Half the continent had changed hands at the scratch of a pen. Governor Bernard, of Massachusetts, proclaimed a day of thanksgiving for the great event, and the Boston newspapers recount how the occasion was celebrated with a parade of the cadets and other volunteer corps, a grand dinner in Faneuil Hall, music, bonfires, illuminations, firing of cannon, and above

all, by sermons in every church of the province; for the heart of early New England always found voice through her pulpits. ...

On the American continent the war was ended, and the British colonists breathed for a space, as they drifted unwittingly towards a deadlier strife.

Thinking Historically

1. How could victory in the French and Indian War lead to "a deadlier strife"?
2. Since many of the indigenous natives stood with France, what do you suppose these people thought about Great Britain's triumph in the conflict?
3. Could the mother country have mended her relationship with her colonists now that France was subdued?
4. Why was England displeased with its American colonies?
5. What problems will arise from the cost of the conflict?

4

REVOLUTION

One of the themes of American history is conflict. It meanders through the centuries, beginning with the arrival of explorers who brutally shoved the indigenous people off their land, claiming the riches of the New World for the monarchs of the Old World. We pondered that clash in an earlier chapter. Conflict over the fertile Ohio River Valley propelled France and Great Britain into a clash that went on for almost a decade, with England in 1763 securing victory and a North American Empire by defeating France and its native allies. By that date, a larger conflict began coming into view: one between our mother country and ourselves. This one had its genesis with the end of the French and Indian War.

Victory in the war with France wrecked the mother country's economy, leaving Great Britain with a suffocating 132,000,000-pound debt. Interest alone on this huge debt would consume half of the national budget. Troops had been sent to North America when hostilities began, exasperating the economic strain. Many Native Americans were angry because France had been a reliable and fair trading partner. Administering the new territory gained in the war would prove to be a logistical nightmare for Britain. Immediately, Parliament passed several pieces of legislation to stabilize the situation.

In 1763, the Proclamation Act drew a boundary line between England's 13 American colonies and the newly acquired real estate gained from France. Colonists, eager for the natural resources of the Ohio River Valley, ignored this act. The following year, the Sugar Act made it clear that revenue was needed to ease the mother country's financial burden. Smuggling of sugar products would be discouraged. The 1764 Currency Act mandated the payment of all debts owed to the central government, and British merchants had to be paid in gold, which was badly needed back home after the war. These acts, as previously noted, were passed by a Parliament in which the Americans had no actual representation, only virtual representation. To the mother country, the colonies were undependable and ungrateful children in need of discipline.

The 1765 far-reaching Stamp Act taxed legal documents, such as deeds and wills, as well as almanacs, calendars, liquor bottles, and decks of playing cards. Unpopular Stamp Act tax collectors, who received a portion of the cost of the required stamps, were tarred and feathered, abused by the Sons of Liberty. A Quartering Act ordered colonists to house British troops stationed far from home to oversee the collection of stamp revenue. Within a year, Benjamin Franklin, popular on both sides of the Atlantic Ocean because of his *Poor Richard's Almanack* and inventions, was sent to London to lobby for repeal of the despised Stamp Act, which was accomplished in 1766 but replaced by the Declaratory Act, proclaiming that in the future, Parliament was to be obeyed.

Revenue raising without an actual Parliamentary voice continued. The 1767 Townshend Acts taxed glass, paint, lead, and tea. This time, the Daughters of Liberty joined colonial males in objecting. By the time these despised acts—except for the tax on tea—were repealed three years later, unrest was sweeping colonies like Massachusetts, where Boston Harbor served as a major commercial hub. The 1770 Boston Massacre, where British troops, searching for part-time jobs, clashed with protesters who had assaulted them with lumps of coal rolled in the snow, sparked the first civilian deaths, African American Crispus Attucks among them. He and his comrades were turned into martyrs by the artwork of silversmith Paul Revere. The mother country seemed to be murdering her own children.

An uneasy calm was swept aside in 1773 with the passage of the Tea Act, benefiting the East India Tea Company and its London friends. This act gave the company a monopoly over the sale of the essential product in the colonies. That December, Bostonians, led by barrel maker Samuel Adams and angry independent tea merchant John Hancock, dumped 342 chests of East India Tea Company leaves into the harbor during the Boston Tea Party while security guards ignored the spectacle. When word reached London, Parliament was not amused and passed the 1774 Intolerable (Coercive) Acts to punish the colony of Massachusetts. The lucrative harbor was closed, and the authorities demanded the arrests of instigators Adams and Hancock, who fled after the protest. The other colonies rallied around Massachusetts, and in their First Continental Congress, delegates, fearful that port cities like Philadelphia and New York might be targeted next, drafted a Declaration of Rights and Grievances, which outlined complaints against England that had been building for a century. Rebuffed by Parliament and King George III, blood was spilled in Lexington and Concord in 1775 as American militia fired on British troops searching for Adams and Hancock.

The First Continental Congress was not yet ready to call for independence, but it created a ragtag army (without a commander) and discussed the estrangement between mother and child. By early 1776, the Congress, which had evolved into a Second Continental Congress, read with interest Thomas Paine's pamphlet "Common Sense," which lamented the attack on liberty by Great Britain. To the delegates, it was becoming clear, as Paine argued, that freedom was being "extinguished" by powerful forces back home. Meeting in Philadelphia, the Congress approved in June 1776 Virginian Richard Henry Lee's resolution calling for independence. Thomas Jefferson and a committee prepared the document, blaming King George for the actions taken by Parliament (see Document 0.2). By early July, Congress, using the literary talents of Jefferson, had taken a dramatic step. The Declaration of Independence eloquently explained to the colonists (Loyalists, Patriots, and undecided), king and Parliament, and the world the justification for independence. It would be a messy and lengthy divorce with George Washington at the helm of the Patriot military.

Watching the fracturing of Britain's American Empire, France, still seething from its loss in the French and Indian War, aided Washington's Continental Army. By the 1777 Battle of Saratoga, the French were supplying invaluable assistance. Even a brutal winter in 1777 through 1778 at Valley Forge could not dampen the revolutionary fervor. Loyalists saw their property confiscated for the war effort. When Charleston fell to the British in 1780 and the Patriots fled the battlefield at Camden, the rebels stood strong at Kings Mountain in October, killing the commander, Major Patrick Ferguson, who had pledged to Britain's Lord Charles Cornwallis to "subdue the rebels." In early 1781, victory at Cowpens followed.

The cost of the war, increasing the debt of the mother country, and the logistics of fighting a trans-Atlantic conflict, created a final battle in 1781 at the peninsula of York-town, where Washington's solders and the French fleet trapped Lord Cornwallis's forces. His surrender led to the 1783 Treaty of Paris, granting independence and Canadian fishing rights to the Americans and calling for compensation for the Loyalists and payment of debts owed to England. The treaty's last two provisions would be ignored by the jubilant victors. As England left America, it took with it African American slaves who had remained loyal to the mother country when fighting began. The conflict had achieved its result: independence had been formalized for Great Britain's 13 American colonies.

Document 4.1. Map of the 13 Colonies in 1776

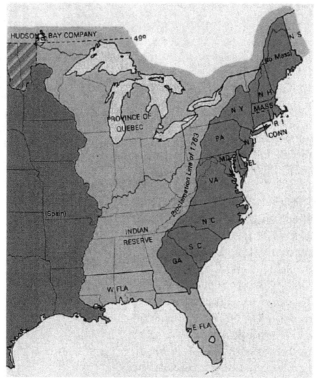

Fig. 4.1: Source: https://commons.wikimedia.org/wiki/File:Map_of_territorial_growth_1775.jpg.

Thinking Historically

1. By studying this map, what sectional differences do you assume existed among Britain's American colonies?
2. Would the new nation be ambitious for further westward growth?
3. After the victory, what challenges would face a nation that stretched from New Hampshire to Georgia?
4. Did France have any ambitions in America of its own?
5. How would the evacuation of Loyalist slaves affect the southern economy?

Document 4.2. The 1766 Declaratory Act

Great Britain's triumph over France created new challenges, especially in the debt created by the French and Indian War. Parliament, as previously noted, enacted legislation without actual representation by its colonists. One of the laws that created friction with the Americans was the far-reaching 1765 Stamp Act. The colonists protested this revenue-raising legislation, and groups of males, the Sons of Liberty, terrorized the Stamp Act tax collectors by tarring and feathering them and in other demonstrations of anger. Meetings in the colonies were convened in opposition to the Stamp Act. After Benjamin Franklin lobbied for the law's repeal, Parliament agreed in 1766 but asserted its control of colonial affairs with the Declaratory Act, excerpted next.

> An act for the better securing the dependency of his Majesty's dominions in America upon the crown and parliament of Great Britain.
>
> Whereas several of the houses of representatives in his Majesty's colonies and plantations in America, have of late, against law, claimed to themselves, or to the general assemblies of the same, the sole and exclusive right of imposing duties and taxes upon his Majesty's subjects in the said colonies and plantations; and have, in pursuance of such claim, passed certain votes, resolutions, and orders, derogatory to the legislative authority of parliament, and inconsistent with the dependency of the said colonies and plantations, and inconsistent with the dependency of said colonies upon the crown of Great Britain ... be it declared ... That the said colonies and plantations in America have been, are, and of right ought to be, subordinate unto, and dependent upon the imperial crown and parliament of Great Britain.

Thinking Historically

1. As the relationship between Parliament and the colonists deteriorated, how do you assess blame?
2. Would actual, rather than virtual representation in Parliament, have prevented the estrangement of the 1760s?

3. Why did the Americans believe they were entitled to better treatment by the government in London?
4. What part of the Declaratory Act did the colonists ignore?
5. Could cooler heads have patched up the deteriorating relationship?

Document 4.3. Patrick Henry's Boldness

Virginia lawyer Patrick Henry addressed the colonies' assembly in 1775. The young orator considered the mother country's actions to be threats to liberty. The deteriorating relationship was created by unfair legislation by England, as described in this chapter, Henry argued. In the excerpt of that speech that follows, he says time for cordial relations between Great Britain and the colonies has passed and peace has been swept aside by war.

> It is vain, sir, to extenuate the matter. The gentlemen may cry, Peace, peace! But there is no peace. The war has actually begun! The next gale that sweeps from the north will bring to our ears the clash of resounding arms! Our brethren are already in the field! Why stand we here idle? What is it that the gentlemen wish? What would they have? Is life so dear or peace so sweet as to be purchased at the price of chains and slavery? Forbid it, almighty God. I know not what course others might take, but as for me, give me liberty or give me death!

Thinking Historically

1. Apparently, there were some colonists advocating peace between Great Britain and the Americans. Who might have been these people?
2. Is Henry correct in laying the blame for the situation at the feet of the mother country?
3. Why was Virginia at the forefront of those colonies calling for a revolution?
4. How had Parliament's description of the colonists as "raw, undisciplined, cowardly men" enflamed passions?
5. In 1775, could cooler heads have stepped forward and extinguished Henry's boldness?

Document 4.4. Thomas Paine's "Common Sense"

By early 1776, much had happened in the accelerating movement for independence. Armed conflict had occurred the year before at Massachusetts battles named "Lexington," "Concord," and "Bunker Hill." Colonists, however, were split over the fundamental question of leaving the British Empire, despite the rhetoric of people like Patrick Henry. Loyalists urged a cooling of passions. In January 1776, however, a newcomer named Thomas Paine published his 47-page pamphlet entitled "Common Sense," which sold 120,000 copies in three months. This excerpt is from that document.

> I have heard it asserted by some that, as America has flourished under her former connection with Great Britain, the same connection is necessary towards her future happiness, and will always have the same effect. Nothing could be more fallacious than this kind of argument. We may as well assert that, because a child has thrived upon milk, it is never to have meat, or that the first twenty years of our lives is to become a precedent for the next twenty. But even this is admitting more than is true. For I answer roundly that America would have flourished as much, and probably much more, had no European power taken any notice of her.

Thinking Historically

1. How do you analyze the deteriorating relationship that began the previous century between mother and child?
2. Is Paine correct in his argument that the situation in 1776 should be "common sense"?
3. What counterargument could Parliament offer to refute Paine's position?
4. Could the colonies have "flourished" without the guidance of the mother country?
5. Do you agree with those who consider Thomas Paine to be an "agitator," stirring up trouble?

Document 4.5. Abigail Adams's 1776 Plea to Her Husband

Abigail and John Adams seem to have spent their entire lives in love. When they were separated by John's service in the Continental Congress, Abigail wrote him daily, inquiring about the deliberations of Congress as a decision on independence loomed. By March, Abigail was concerned that a declaration might omit an improvement in the status of women. In the following excerpt, Abigail, writing from Quincy, Massachusetts, pleads with John in Philadelphia for gender equality. Interestingly, he responds by writing to his beloved wife, "Keep your saucy comments to yourself."

> I long to hear that you have declared an independency—and by the new Code of Laws which I suppose it will be necessary for you to make I desire that you would Remember the Ladies, and be more generous and favorable to them than your ancestors. Do not put such unlimited power into the hands of the Husbands. Remember all Men would be tyrants if they could. If particular care and attention is not paid to the Ladies we are determined

to foment a Rebellion, and will not hold ourselves bound by any Laws in which we have no voice or Representation.

Thinking Historically

1. If one of the causes of the Revolution was the question of representation, does Abigail make a valid point about 50 percent of the colonial population?
2. The Founding Fathers were males; does excluding females limit their understanding of what America should be?
3. Why would John object to his wife's plea?
4. What, exactly, will the Declaration's statement "all men are created equal" mean?
5. Why would women be denied equal political power until 1920 and the ratification of the Nineteenth Amendment?

Document 4.6. The Human Cost of War

Comparatively, the American Revolution's death totals were far lower than later wars, for instance, the Vietnam War, which cost 58,000 American lives. The 8,000 combat lives lost, however, fail to reveal the pain of 25,000 wounded and Loyalists who had their lives ruined by the conflict because of their allegiance to the Crown. In fact, 17,000 Americans died of "other" causes than combat. The misery of war was on display in places like Valley Forge, Pennsylvania, during the winter of 1777 to 1778. In the following excerpt, a Connecticut physician, Albigence Waldo, describes some of the human cost of the war.

> December 14—Prisoners and Deserters are continually coming in. The Army which has been surprisingly healthy hitherto, now begins to grow sickly from the continued fatigues they have suffered this Campaign. Yet they still show a spirit of Alarcity & Contentment not to be expected from so young Troops. I am Sick-discontented—and out of humour. Poor food-hard lodging—Cold Weather-fatigue—Nasty Cloaths-nasty Cookery—Vomit half my time—smoak'd out of my senses—the Devil's in't—I can't Endure it—Why are we sent here to starve and Freeze—What sweet Felicities have I left at home; A charming Wife—pretty Children—Good Beds—good food-good Cookery—all agreeable—all harmonious. Here all Confusion—smoke and Cold—hunger & filthiness—A pox on my bad luck.

Thinking Historically

1. Are Dr. Waldo's experiences unique to the American Revolution?
2. Were the British at Valley Forge not enduring the same hardships?
3. How will this brutal winter strengthen the American Army's resolve?

4. Did the fact that George and Martha Washington also camped with their troops that winter send a positive message to the army?
5. Under these terrible conditions, why did the Continental Army not surrender?

Document 4.7. Lord Dunmore's Proclamation

In November 1775, John Murray, Earl of Dunmore and royal governor of Virginia, issued a proclamation that bears his name. By that time, the Americans and British had clashed at Lexington, Concord, and Bunker Hill. Blood had been shed, but independence had not been declared. Lord Dunmore, anticipating a broadening of the conflict, promised any slave who remained loyal to the Crown would receive his/her freedom. After the colonies achieved their independence with the 1783 Treaty of Paris, Lord Dunmore's Proclamation, excerpted below, would be honored as British troops left America, an action that drew criticism from George Washington.

> As I have ever entertained Hopes that an Accommodation might take Place between Great-Britain and this Colony, without being compelled by my Duty to this most disagreeable but now absolutely necessary Step, rendered so by a Body of armed men unlawfully assembled, firing on His Majesty's Tenders, and the Formation of an army, and the army now on their March to attack His Majesty's Troops and destroy the well disposed Subjects of the Colony. ...
>
> ... I do hereby farther declare all indentured Servants, Negroes, or others ... free that are able and willing to bear Arms, they joining His Majesty's Troops as soon as may be, from the more speedily reducing this Colony to a proper Sense of Duty, to His Majesty's Crown and Dignity.

Thinking Historically

1. How did Lord Dunmore, writing seven months before the Declaration of Independence, understand the dimensions of the coming war?
2. What, exactly, were the royal governor's objectives?
3. Why did he not fear emancipating the slaves?
4. At war's end, why did George Washington, a Virginia slave owner, object to the fulfillment of Dunmore's pledge?
5. What does the honoring of this proclamation in 1783, tell us about our former mother country?

5

POSTERITY

With independence achieved, the 13 states operated under the Articles of Confederation, a loose association with no president, federal judiciary, mandatory taxes, or central authority. To pass legislation, the states had to agree unanimously, and little was accomplished in what historian John Fiske called "the critical period." We were a weak government, suspicious of creating a system that might give too much power to an elite. No one was in charge; Congress, lacking money, stumbled along. Watching this situation was our ex-mother country; France, which had assisted our bid for independence; and Spain, which controlled Florida.

When Daniel Shays, a Massachusetts farmer and Revolutionary War officer, protested in 1786 against the state courts for foreclosing on his farm, he was joined by other angry citizens like himself. The state court system was impotent; the central government was paralyzed. Representing America in France as our ambassador Thomas Jefferson, who observed of Shays' Rebellion, "A little rebellion now and then is a good thing." More alarmed and closer to the scene, George Washington wrote, "I fear a gradual unravelling of things." To Washington, Shays' Rebellion was indicative of the weakness of the central government and its Articles of Confederation. Congress called in the spring of 1787 for an effort to "revise" the Articles of Confederation.

Realizing the dire situation facing the new nation, the delegates to this Philadelphia meeting ignored "revision" and commenced in secrecy to draft what would become by September the US Constitution. Southern representatives wanted to protect slavery, while those from New York and Massachusetts saw the value of a strong government. Leading figures at this convention were George Washington (the chair), James Madison of Virginia, New York's Alexander Hamilton, and Pennsylvania's Benjamin Franklin, who had witnessed so much in his eight decades. Hamilton wanted a strong central government and financial strength. The southerners would not support any proposal that threatened the human basis of their agricultural system.

Arguments between big states, small states, slave states, free states, agricultural states, and industrial states demanded the talents of George Washington, who historian James Flexner calls "the indispensable man," and others, like Madison, who worked to produce an acceptable compromise. Checks and balances between government branches were created. Slaves were deemed to be three-fifths of a person. Anti-federalists, fearful of the creation of a new monarch who would trample on liberty, called for the protection of human rights. Throughout the summer of 1787, the delegates worked on a document that would replace the Articles of Confederation with a form of government in which all states had certain powers but would operate under a strong central authority, without a King but with taxing authority. The compromise created a president, a federal court system, and a bicameral congress sensitive to large and small states. The framers avoided the divisive issue of slavery, except for agreeing that importation of Africans would cease in 1808.

After the document was completed, Congress prepared to send the Constitution to the states for consideration. For the next year, supporters of the document's ratification, led by Madison, Hamilton, and John Jay, rallied around a series of newspaper articles they authored called *The Federalist Papers*. Understood was the need to placate the concerns of the anti-federalists, who worried about giving too much power to the central government. Among the anti-federalists were Patrick Henry, Samuel Adams, and Richard Henry Lee, key figures from the American Revolution.

By 1789, the Constitution had been ratified by the states. A Bill of Rights protecting individual liberties was promised to the anti-federalists and would be added to the Constitution in 1791. Weakness was replaced with strength. The delegates throughout the process kept their eyes on "posterity," the future. The new document, and its Bill of Rights, produced a president, George Washington; a vice president, John Adams; and a team of advisers, which, although not specifically mentioned in the Constitution, we call "the cabinet." Chief among these would be Secretary of State Thomas Jefferson and Secretary of the Treasury Alexander Hamilton. A system of congressional representation fair to all states (each state received two senators, and House of Representatives membership was based on population) and a supreme court were in the Constitution. Differences remained among the sections, however, and an opportunity to end human bondage was missed by the framers. The Republic's "posterity" would be threatened by these unresolved issues and the tensions that erupted in the Civil War of the early 1860s.

Document 5.1. The Articles of Confederation

After independence was declared, Congress put in place the Articles of Confederation, a weak system of government that retained state sovereignty. The American Revolution was fought under this system, and it was formally approved by Congress in 1781. It was this flawed confederacy, lacking a vibrant central authority, as well as financial resources, which was in place when Daniel Shays, a Massachusetts farmer and officer from the Revolution, paralyzed the court system of Massachusetts in 1786 during Shays' Rebellion. The following are excerpts from the Articles of Confederation.

Art. II. Each state retains its sovereignty, freedom and independence, and every Power, Jurisdiction and right, which is not by this confederation expressly delegated to the United States, in Congress assembled.

Art. IX. The united states in congress assembled shall also be the last resort on appeal in all disputes and differences now subsisting or that hereafter may arise between two or more states concerning boundary, jurisdiction or any other cause whatever; ...

Art. XI. Canada acceding to this confederation, and joining in the measures of the united states, shall be admitted into, and entitled to all the advantages of this union.

Thinking Historically

1. What, exactly, is a "confederacy" and why is it a fundamentally flawed system of government?
2. In the Articles of Confederation, why is Congress the only branch of government?
3. Why was state sovereignty important to the framers of this document?
4. Was Congress's wish that Canada might join the United States realistic?
5. How did this weak confederacy hamper the response to the 1786 Shays' Rebellion?

Document 5.2. George Washington's 1786 View

Shays' Rebellion alarmed Virginia's George Washington, who feared that such events might undermine the young nation. In the excerpt that follows, written in December 1786, Washington writes General Henry Knox, who had served as the Revolution's chief of artillery and in the Confederation government, about his concerns.

That G(reat) B(retain) will be an unconcerned Spectator of the present insurrections (if they continue) is not to be expected. That she is at this moment sowing the Seeds of jealousy and discontent among the various tribes of Indians on our frontier admits of no doubt, in my mind. And that she will improve every opportunity to foment the spirit of turbulence within the bowels of the United States, with a view of distracting our governments, and promoting divisions, is, with me, not less certain.

Thinking Historically

1. Why does George Washington believe that Great Britain will exploit the weakness created by Shays' Rebellion?
2. Is Washington justified in seeing a partnership between Native Americans and our former mother country?

3. Why did Thomas Jefferson, serving in France, see Shays' Rebellion as merely "turbulence"?
4. How would Washington's view of the situation lead to the convening of a meeting to "revise" the Articles of Confederation?
5. Why would the delegates attempt to "replace" instead of merely "revise" the system that Washington described?

Document 5.3. The Constitution's Preamble

As this chapter reminds us, the delegates to the 1787 Constitutional Convention compromised among themselves. Big states, small states, agricultural states, manufacturing states, northern states, and southern states sought common ground that would correct the weaknesses of the Confederacy and create a strong central government. The Constitution's preamble clearly states the delegates' goals.

> We The People of the United States, in Order to form a more perfect Union, establish Justice, insure domestic Tranquility, provide for the common defence, promote the general Welfare, and secure the Blessings of Liberty to ourselves and our Posterity, do ordain and establish this Constitution for the United States of America.

Thinking Historically

1. What "people of the United States" were excluded from the protections of this document?
2. How would you define the goal of "a more perfect Union"?
3. Why is "domestic Tranquility" important to the Constitution's framers?
4. Define "the general Welfare."
5. Why is the document's emphasis on "Posterity" important?

Document 5.4. James Madison's 1788 Defense of Factions

As mentioned in this chapter, James Madison, Alexander Hamilton, and John Jay will step forward during the ratification debate and produce 85 newspaper articles known as *The Federalist Papers* to try to persuade the states to approve the Constitution. *Federalist* no. 10 was written by James Madison. In this essay, Madison seeks to reduce fears of factions. He believes the new Constitution with its Republican government will harness the energy of factions while also sidestepping the destructive features of them.

If a faction consists of less than a majority, relief is supplied by the republican principle, which enables the majority to defeat its sinister views by regular vote. It may clog the administration, it may convulse the society; but it will be unable to execute and mask its violence under the forms of the Constitution. When a majority is included in a faction, the form of popular government, on the other hand, enables it to sacrifice to its ruling passion or interest both the public good and the rights of the citizens. To secure the public good and private rights against the danger of such a faction, and at the same time to preserve the spirit and the form of popular government, is then the great object to which our inquiries are directed.

Thinking Historically

1. As a large nation, even in 1788, how could the differences among factions strengthen the Republic?
2. What factions, other than the North and South, existed in America at this time?
3. Does Madison believe the Constitution will avoid the divisions of various factions?
4. When do factions pose a clear threat to a Republic?
5. Why will Madison's view triumph in the ratification process?

Document 5.5. The First Amendment

The anti-federalists argued strongly for a written guarantee of basic human rights. While they boycotted the Constitutional Convention, many of these people had fought for independence, and their voices were heard during the ratification debates. Thus, to calm the anti-federalists' concerns about a strong central government that might be tempted to trample on the liberties of individuals, a Bill of Rights became the first ten amendments to the Constitution in 1791. The following is the First Amendment.

> Congress shall make no law respecting an establishment of religion, or prohibiting the free exercise thereof; or abridging the freedom of speech, or of the press; or the right of the people peaceable to assemble, and to petition the Government for a redress of grievances.

Thinking Historically

1. Why does this amendment specifically restrict Congress?
2. Do memories of the powerful official church of Great Britain persuade the Republic to assert freedom of religion?
3. Why are freedom of speech and the press important to the anti-federalists?
4. Are there limitations to freedom of speech and press?
5. Why are assembly and petition fundamental American rights?

6

REPUBLIC

Respect for George Washington's essential role as military commander during the Revolution and as chair of the critical Constitutional Convention did not prevent quarrels between Secretary of State Thomas Jefferson and Secretary of the Treasury Alexander Hamilton. The latter proposed a strong financial plan in 1791 for the new government with a national bank, even though the Constitution did not mention such a measure. Jefferson, sensing a bias by the manufacturing states like Hamilton's New York, advocated a strict or narrow interpretation of the Constitution; Hamilton considered a bank "necessary and proper" for the Republic's financial vitality.

In 1794, when western Pennsylvania farmers objected to taxes on grain, the Whiskey Rebellion was extinguished by the threat of military force, with Washington and Hamilton in the forefront. The two cabinet secretaries also favored opposing sides in the ongoing war between Britain and France, the latter backed by Jefferson. Washington resisted this foreign entanglement when France tried to arrange a meeting with an emissary, citizen Edmond Genet, in 1793. Frustrated, Jefferson, believing that the agricultural states lacked influence in the administration, left government that year and contemplated future challenges.

Political parties began to emerge during Washington's second term, even though the president objected. Jefferson and his Virginia ally James Madison led the Democratic-Republicans with Vice President John Adams and Hamilton leading the Federalists, despite Washington's Farewell Address in 1796, which warned against partisanship and foreign alliances. That year, Adams succeeded Washington as president, and Jefferson became vice president. At that time, the Constitution did not prohibit partisan splits such as this one that was destined to aggravate the political situation. Both leaders appealed to different constituencies and advocated different interpretations of the Constitution, as well as conflicting views of the continuing war between Britain and France. In 1797, Adams rebuffed efforts by France to gain support during the XYZ Affair.

Bubbling over to Congress, scuffles occurred in 1798 over the Alien and Sedition Acts, legislation that made it difficult for immigrants, who supported the

Democratic-Republicans, to obtain citizenship and restricted criticism of President Adams. The Jeffersonians argued that the First Amendment to the Constitution, part of the Bill of Rights (see Document 5.5) protected free speech and press. A close election in 1800 produced the Republic's first transfer of power, peaceful but divisive and personal, with Jefferson and his allies narrowly winning.

In the final days of the Adams administration, the outgoing president appointed Federalists to various offices, including William Marbury as justice of the peace of the District of Columbia. The dispute over these "midnight appointments" resulted in the landmark 1803 Supreme Court decision *Marbury v. Madison*. The court sympathized with Marbury but ruled that he had sued under an unconstitutional act of Congress (the Judiciary Act). Thus the principle of "judicial review" became a powerful tool for the court. Acts of Congress could be scrutinized by the Supreme Court.

Jefferson abandoned his strict interpretation of the Constitution in 1803 when he authorized the $15,000,000 purchase of Louisiana from France's Napoleon, doubling the size of our country and illustrating the theme of national growth, as well as removing foreign presence from America's borders. Supporting Jefferson's bold action, the voters reelected him in 1804, the same year that Hamilton was mortally wounded in a duel with Vice President Aaron Burr. Jefferson's popularity was diminished in 1807, however, when Britain "impressed" (kidnapped) American sailors off the coast of Virginia in American waters. The Democratic-Republicans responded to this provocation by passing the Embargo Act of that year, ceasing any foreign trade and subsequently wrecking the north's manufacturing economy. Two years later, as Jefferson prepared to leave the White House, the Embargo Act was replaced with the 1809 Non-Intercourse Act, preventing trade with just warring Britain and France. Northern states, dependent on foreign trade, contemplated secession.

By the time James Madison assumed the presidency, friction between the United States and our former mother country was exacerbated by Congress's "war hawks," leaders who favored another conflict with Britain and possible expansion into Canada. Chief among these agitators were South Carolina's John C. Calhoun and Kentucky's Henry Clay. The War of 1812 was a dismal failure for the United States; Canada did not wish to become part of America's empire. British soldiers, who had defeated France's Napoleon, burned the White House and other public buildings in 1814. The Treaty of Ghent ended the war and failed to give us Canada or to prohibit impressment. After the agreement was signed, in early 1815, General Andrew Jackson soundly defeated the British who had not yet evacuated, killing 2,000 troops and earning for himself the nickname "Hero of New Orleans," one of the bright moments in the Republic's first decades as Americans sought to define our national destiny.

Document 6.1. First Lady Abigail Adams View of the New Capital, 1800

The Adams family would be the first occupants of the White House. The nation's capital city had been created in space ceded by the southern states of Maryland and Virginia. The excerpt that follows gives us her impressions of a city that would rise in the wilderness of the new Republic.

> Yesterday I returned fifteen visits,—but such a place as Georgetown appears,—why, our Milton is beautiful. But no comparisons;—if they will put me up some bells, and let me have wood enough to keep fires, I design to be pleased. I could content myself almost anywhere three months; but, surrounded with forests, can you believe that wood is not to be had, because people cannot be found to cut and cart it! Briesler entered into a contract with a man to supply him with wood. A small part, a few cords only, has he been able to get. Most of that was expended to dry the walls of the house before we came in, and yesterday the man told him it was impossible for him to procure it to be cut and carted. He has had recourse to coals; but we cannot get grates made and set. We have, indeed, come into a NEW COUNTRY.

Thinking Historically

1. Why was this wilderness selected as the site for America's new capital city?
2. Ironically, the Adams family would occupy the unfinished house for only a few months. Why?
3. How is the unfinished city symbolic of the Republic itself?
4. With the pending transfer of power from the Federalists to the Democratic-Republicans, was the environment better suited to the latter political party?
5. Was Washington, DC, the ideal capital of America's new rulers?

With the Adams family sent back to Massachusetts in political defeat, Thomas Jefferson boldly placed his brand on the Republic. The purchase of Louisiana from France's Napoleon allowed him to illustrate his commitment to growth, even when it conflicted with his "strict" interpretation of presidential power. The following map illustrates the enormity of the Louisiana Purchase, which doubled the Republic's size for $15,000,000.

Document 6.2. Map of America, 1803

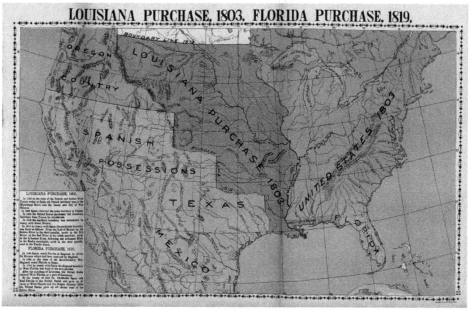

Fig. 6.1: Source: https://www.loc.gov/resource/g3701sm.gct00482/?sp=21.

Thinking Historically

1. Explain how Jefferson believed this acquisition was a legal exercise of presidential power?
2. Why did America's electorate endorse the president's purchase in 1804?
3. What problems did Jefferson create for himself with this action?
4. Did this purchase raise the possibility of further westward growth?
5. Was this growth in keeping with the new Republic's view of itself?

Document 6.3. Native Americans and the Republic's Ambitions

Native Americans attempted to sound the alarms about the Republic's westward growth. They considered the Louisiana Purchase and subsequent colonization to be a threat to their autonomy and culture. Since 1492, the natives had experienced a constriction of their land by greedy European powers who sliced off pieces of this land. As we have seen, many favored France in the French and Indian War, and now the Americans had stretched their presence far into the continent's interior. The following excerpt is the 1812 statement by a pair of native brothers, Lalawethika and Tecumseh.

> The Great Spirit bids me to say to you thus. My children! Have very little to do (with the Americans). They proceeded from the froth of the Great

Lake (Atlantic Ocean) when it was troubled, and wer To them I gave e driven on shore by a strong east wind.—They are very numerous. But I hate them—Because They Take Away Your Lands, which were not made for them—the Whites I placed on the other side of the Great Water, to be another people, separate from you. To them I gave different manners, customs, animals, and vegetables. You may salute them; but must not shake hands.

My children! You must not get drunk. It displeases the Great Spirit. And on no account drink Whiskey. It was made by the Big Knives, without my permission. It makes you sick, and burns your insides. It destroys you.

Thinking Historically

1. Why did the Republic respond to these pleas with military action?
2. Why were the natives' statements of friendship and landownership ignored by the whites?
3. What does the warning about alcohol abuse tell us about the two cultures as they interacted on the frontier?
4. Explain how the natives and the Americans differed on the question of landownership.
5. Can you see the seeds of Indian removal being sown in the aftermath of the Louisiana Purchase?

Document 6.4. President Madison Calls for War

The causes of the War of 1812 were shaped by continued hard feelings between the Republic and our former mother country. The issue of impressment of American sailors by British ships, such as the 1807 incident off the coast of Virginia, illustrates the fact that to many Americans, a forceful response was justified. The Embargo Act and the Non-Intercourse Act, however, wrecked our economy, creating sectional tensions, and did not persuade Britain to cease impressment. Thus with pressure from the Congress's war hawks, lingering hatred for Britain, territorial ambitions, and fear of Native American attacks, James Madison called for a declaration of war. Two years later, no Canadian territory had been gained, much of Washington had been burned, and no cessation of impressment had occurred. But "the Hero of New Orleans," General Jackson, had been created. The following excerpt is President Madison's 1812 request for war.

In reviewing the conduct of Great Britain toward the United States, our attention is necessarily drawn to the warfare just renewed by the savages on one of our extensive frontiers—a warfare which is known to spare neither age nor sex and to be distinguished by features peculiarity shocking to humanity. It is difficult to account for the activity and combinations which have for some time been developing themselves among tribes in constant intercourse with British traders and garrisons, without connecting their hostility with that influence, and without recollecting the authenticated examples of such interpositions heretofore furnished by the officers and agents of that government.

Thinking Historically

1. Explain our nation's reasons for going to war in 1812.
2. Why were there still hard feelings between our Republic and Great Britain?
3. Was the annexation of Canada a realistic expectation?
4. What role did Native American attacks play in Madison's request?
5. How did Andrew Jackson's actions after the war was technically over give rise to a new political force in America?

7

DESTINY

Genneral Andrew Jackson's questionable actions in New Orleans became a proud rallying point for Americans; we had demonstrated our formidable strength, even if it was after the peace treaty had been signed, which ended the War of 1812. As we will see, war hawks John C. Calhoun and Henry Clay continued to play prominent roles in our nation for decades, and the charred White House would be rebuilt. We entered the Era of Good Feelings, unifying behind President James Monroe (elected 1820) and building canals like the Erie Canal, which sliced across New York, transporting settlers to the Great Lakes. Roads, Henry Clay's National (Cumberland) Road, took us further into the continent, which, we believed, was our destiny to conquer, no matter what Native Americans might assert. We minimized partisanship and purchased Florida from Spain in 1819 without a shot being fired. But we avoided solving the slavery question by enacting the 1820 Missouri Compromise, which admitted slave state Missouri to the Union while Maine entered as free soil. Case closed on that issue, we thought.

In 1823, the president issued the Monroe Doctrine, proclaiming to the world that the Western Hemisphere was *our* domain; foreign nations could not establish American colonies. If they violated this dictate, we would consider that action "serious." Left unsaid was what we would actually do about such violations. Throughout the Era of Good Feelings, the United States moved forward, avoiding the issue of human bondage, which decades later would rip our country apart.

The Hero of New Orleans returned to Tennessee, disavowing any interest in politics. John Quincy Adams, the son of former president John Adams, made his intentions known in 1824. He represented the North's manufacturing and banking interests, believing an elite should guide the nation. Other candidates were Speaker of the United States House of Representatives Henry Clay, Georgia's pro-slavery William Crawford, and the champion of the common man, Andrew Jackson, who received the most votes. The Corrupt Bargain of 1824 robbed the Hero of New Orleans of the presidency, however, with Adams and Clay uniting and Adams appointing Clay secretary of state. A bitter rematch between Jackson and Adams four years later, with personal accusations, ended with Jackson's success.

As Jackson, grieving the death of his wife who had been criticized in the campaign, arrived in the nation's capital, the tensions over slavery became obvious. A former slave, David Walker, published "The Appeal" in 1829, urging enslaved people to rise in a bloody insurrection. Asking for freedom, Walker asserted, would be fruitless. Bostonian William Lloyd Garrison published *The Liberator* two years later, an abolitionist newspaper that took aim at the immorality and injustice of slavery. The same year, Virginia slave Nat Turner launched a rebellion, which further revealed the evil of a cruel system that formed the basis of the South's economy and society. It had become an addiction for the planter elite and their white supporters.

A strong personality, Jackson avoided a split in the Union during his tenure. He wrestled with Calhoun over the protective tariff, supported by northern industries. The South Carolinian responded in 1832 with nullification, a belief that acts of Congress, such as the tariff that benefited the north, could be ignored by the agricultural South. Obviously, divisions among the sections were economic as well as societal. In 1832, Jackson objected to the rechartering of the Bank of the United States, which he labeled "a monster" because it made borrowing money difficult for southern and western farmers. Promoting himself as the friend of hard-working people, the president sought to move Native Americans out of the way of ambitious settlers. This Indian removal was brutal and violated court decisions. To Jackson, America belonged to the common man, the common *white* man. It reached a climax in 1838 under his successor, Martin Van Buren, who shoved the Cherokee Indian Nation on the Trail of Tears to Oklahoma. Additionally, Jackson's veto of the Bank of the United States created pet banks, weak financial institutions that collapsed in the Panic of 1837, just as Van Buren became president.

By 1840, the United States eyed Texas, where transplanted Americans had been fighting for their independence from Mexico for five years. Jackson and Van Buren had avoided this issue because it would raise the question of slave expansion and upset the precarious balance in Congress between slave and free states. Abolitionists saw Texas as territory where southerners would grow cotton with slave labor. The decade began with the election of a Whig president, 68-year-old William Henry Harrison. He and his vice president, John Tyler, would face the explosive Texas question. But Harrison died 30 days after his 1841 inauguration, and the country would be confronted with defining its destiny in a war with Mexico.

Document 7.1. The 1823 Monroe Doctrine

As this chapter notes, European encroachment in the Western Hemisphere alarmed America. Russians were drifting southward from Alaska into California, and Great Britain always worried the United States. With the help of Secretary of State John Quincy Adams, President James Monroe alerted Europe to the dimensions of the American Empire. Ultimately, the Monroe Doctrine, excerpted next, became a cornerstone of our foreign policy.

Our policy in regard to Europe, which was adopted at an early stage of the wars which have so long agitated that quarter of the globe, nevertheless remains the same, which is, not to interfere in the internal concerns of any of its powers; to consider the government *de facto* as the legitimate government for us; to cultivate friendly relations with it, and to preserve those relations by a frank, firm, and manly policy, meeting in all instances the just claims of every power, submitting to injuries from none. But in regard to these continents circumstances are eminently and conspicuously different. It is impossible that the allied powers should extend their political system to any portion of either continent without endangering our peace and happiness.

Thinking Historically

1. How was the Monroe Doctrine received by the nations, "the allied powers," of Europe?
2. What, exactly, worried President Monroe about European encroachment in the Western Hemisphere?
3. While weak in enforcement, how did this proclamation legitimize our Western Hemisphere territorial claims?
4. Is Monroe articulating American separateness and exceptionalism?
5. How will the Monroe Doctrine be applied to our hemisphere after 1823?

Document 7.2. Indian Removal in the 1830s

Expansion is a theme that flows through our nation's history. Native Americans, such as the Cherokees, tried to accommodate the presence of white settlers by adopting a constitution, allowing the presence of Christian missionaries, signing agreements with our governments, and suing in our courts. By 1830, however, Indian removal was underway, led by President Jackson and his allies. The following is a portion of the "Appeal of the Cherokee Nation."

We are aware that some persons suppose that it will be for our advantage to remove beyond the Mississippi. We think otherwise. ...

We are not willing to remove; and if we could be brought to this extremity, it would be, not by argument; not because our judgment was satisfied; not because our condition will be improved—but only because we cannot endure to be deprived of our national and individual rights, and subjected to a process of intolerable oppression.

Thinking Historically

1. In your opinion, how did President Jackson justify his Indian removal policy?
2. Why did even favorable court decisions not end this policy?

3. Did Jackson's strong personality and use of the military assure his ultimate success?
4. How else could the Native Americans have responded to their removal?
5. Did this 1830 effort at removal guarantee the eventual Trail of Tears for the Cherokee Nation?

Document 7.3. A Slave Woman Remembers

The system of human bondage, which began with the arrival of Africans in the 1600s, was brutal. Insurrections occurred in the 1700s and 1800s. As this chapter notes, by the 1830s, abolitionists and pro-slavery advocates were arguing their viewpoints, and publications like *The Liberator* were documenting the system's injustice. The Texas question, mentioned in this chapter, would sharpen the national debate. In the 1930s, the New Deal sponsored interviews with former slaves. The following is an example of these interviews.

> But old Boss Jones had a mean overseer who took advantage of the women in the fields. One time he slammed a [n-----] woman down that was heavy, and caused her to have her baby-dead. The [n-----] women in the quarters jumped on him and said they werer going to take him to a brushpile and burn him up. But their men hollered for them to turn him loose. Then Big Boss Jones came and made the women go back to the quarters. He said, "I ain't whipped these wretches for a long time, and I aim to whip them this evening." But all the women hid in the woods that evening, and Boss never said any more about it.
>
> Yes, I saw a [n-----] in chains once. He was my mammy's brother. He stole the house girl and ran off with her to Camden (South Carolina). Big Boss brought him back, whipped him, and kept him chained in the kitchen for two weeks. Every morning Boss would go to the kitchen and whip him again.

Thinking Historically

1. How are memories such as this useful to us as students of the system of slavery?
2. How does this account depict the experience of female slaves?
3. How, exactly, could southern governments defend the brutality of slavery?
4. What kind of emotional and/or intellectual response do you have when you read this account, today?
5. By the 1830s, the system of human bondage had become the most divisive issue facing our nation. Why?

Document 7.4. Jackson and the Nullifiers

As this chapter mentions, debate over economic development created sharp opinions in the industrialized North and the agricultural South. President Jackson saw benefit in a protective tariff which encouraged citizens to purchase goods manufactured here. John C. Calhoun, who served as Jackson's vice president for a while, as well as serving earlier as John Q. Adams' vice president, saw the tariff to be discriminatory against the South. Emotions ran high on the tariff issue with Calhoun's home state of South Carolina staking out the position that individual states could "nullify" or ignore federal laws. The following is South Carolina's 1832 answer to Jackson's threat to "force" adherence to the tariff.

> Resolved, That the power vested by the Constitution and laws in the President of the United States, to issue his proclamation, does not authorize him in that mode, to interfere whenever he may think fit, in the affairs of the respective states, or that he should use it as a means of promulgating executive expositions of the Constitution, with the sanction of force thus superseding the action of other departments of the general government.

Thinking Historically

1. Analyze the president's interpretation of his executive authority concerning the tariff.
2. Analyze Calhoun's states' rights position.
3. Which leader had our national interest at heart? Why?
4. Was a tariff essential for our nation's economic health?
5. How did we avoid a Civil War over this issue in 1832?

8

POISON

John Tyler, an anti-Jackson Democrat who lacked Whig Party credentials, ran into problems immediately. His entire Whig cabinet, except for Secretary of State Daniel Webster, resigned when Harrison, who had appointed them, died in April 1841. Some people suggested that Tyler was only temporarily president, but he saw it differently. His view of presidential succession became a fundamental principle. The festering problem of Texas, which had declared its independence from Mexico in 1835, was foremost on the members of Congress's minds. For more than five years, courageous Texans, many with ties to the United States, had been battling the Mexican army at places like the Alamo and San Jacinto. They had pled with Jackson and Van Buren for assistance, but those presidents had dodged the issue of annexation because it would focus attention on slavery expansion and upset the balance in Congress between free and slave state representation.

Tyler, an "accidental" president to his opponents, was largely ignored until in 1844, shortly before he left office, he urged Congress to accept Texas into the Union. This action was sure to trigger war with Mexico, which had tried to negotiate a peaceful solution to the Texas question. In fact, Texas was forefront in that year's presidential campaign between Whig Henry Clay, who had shifting views on Texas, and Democrat James K. Polk, who articulated "re-annexation," the belief that the territory had actually been part of Thomas Jefferson's enormous 1803 Louisiana Purchase. That position, coupled with an aggressive stance on the Oregon border dispute with British Canada, won Polk the White House in 1844. War with Mexico appeared inevitable despite Mexico's willingness to sell most of Texas, north of the Nueces River, to the United States. Prior to leaving office, John Tyler and Congress added Texas to our country via a joint resolution. Thus, as Polk assumed the presidency, the stage was set for conflict.

Polk, a North Carolinian who had moved to Tennessee, had become a disciple of Andrew Jackson, who himself was born in South Carolina before moving west. Jackson was "Old Hickory," and Polk was "Young Hickory." Both men were shrewd political operatives with a keen understanding of what journalist John O'Sullivan had called "Manifest Destiny." America's "destiny" since its birth had been to sweep across the continent, tossing aside anyone who interfered with this goal: Native

Americans or Mexicans. "Young Hickory's" mission, therefore, was to fulfill America's "destiny."

The poet Ralph Waldo Emerson observed that America's superior military, with its navy and strong leadership, would triumph in battle, but the poet cautioned: "Mexico will poison us." His warning made clear that increasing our territory, one of the themes that meander through our history, would reopen the discussion of slavery expansion. Polk, seeking war, sent General Zachary Taylor in 1846 into a tense area between the Nueces and Rio Grande Rivers, despite objections from Mexico. American troops were killed in a clash; Polk requested a congressional declaration of war because "American blood has been spilled on American soil." House of Representatives member Abraham Lincoln of Illinois tried unsuccessfully to get Polk to identify "the spot" where the bloodshed had occurred. The Congress ignored Lincoln's "spot resolution." War fever had taken hold in the capital.

From 1846 through 1848, American troops marched into Mexico and the southwest, fulfilling our destiny as they scaled the walls of Mexico City and "liberated" California. By the 1848 Treaty of Guadalupe Hidalgo, Americans had gained an enormous amount of territory, stretching from Texas to California, but it would, indeed, "poison" us.

Victory in 1848 was followed that year by the Women's Declaration of Sentiments (see Document 0.3), an eloquent document that promoted gender equality, another theme in our history. Ironically, this request was well-received but put on hold while national leaders debated whether the new territory would be free or slave. Other reform initiatives arose in the decade: Horace Mann's views on education and Dorothea Dix's concern for the insane and inmates, for example. Overshadowing these endeavors, however, was the "poison" of Mexico.

Document 8.1. President Polk's 1846 War Message

For a decade (from 1835 through 1846) presidents had avoided the pleas of transplanted Americans who lived in the Mexican Empire for annexation. Jackson and Van Buren wished to upset the balance between free and slave states in the Congress. The unexpected death of William Henry Harrison in 1841 and the assumption of executive powers by Tyler, however, created a political climate ripe for aggression and annexation. The following is an excerpt from Polk's 1846 request to Congress for war.

> In making these recommendations I deem it proper to declare that it is my anxious desire not only to terminate hostilities speedily, but to bring all matters in dispute between this Government and Mexico to an early and amicable adjustment and in this view I shall be prepared to renew negotiations whenever Mexico shall be ready to receive propositions or to make propositions of her own.

Thinking Historically

1. What response did Polk expect from the Congress for his request to avenge hostilities between the Nueces and Rio Grande Rivers?
2. What response did he expect from the Mexican government?
3. Explain Polk's use of the word "propositions" in his war message.
4. Does Polk fail to grasp that victory would "poison" us by opening a vigorous debate over slavery expansion?
5. Was Polk leaving no peaceful options open to Mexico?

Document 8.2. Map of War with Mexico

Fig. 8.1: Source: https://commons.wikimedia.org/wiki/File:U.S._Territorial_Acquisitions.png.

As this chapter makes clear, Americans under the leadership of President Polk hungered to fulfill our territorial destiny. There was almost a religious fervor to this goal. This map illustrates the growth that would occur in a war with Mexico, expanding the United States from Texas to the Pacific Ocean. This growth, however, would lead to a much larger conflict: the Civil War.

Thinking Historically

1. How could this conflict have been avoided?
2. Why was Representative Lincoln's "spot" question ignored?
3. How, exactly, will victory against Mexico "poison" our nation?

4. Analyze the effect Manifest Destiny had on our relations with Mexico.
5. Was there an "antidote" available for the "poison"?

Document 8.3. Dorothea Dix's 1843 Appeal

Seeds of reform were being planted by courageous crusaders like Boston schoolteacher Dorothea Dix. In 1843, she stepped forward to ask legislators to improve conditions in facilities for the treatment of the insane. One of her objectives was the protection of the insane in facilities where they often fell prey to the convict population. The following is an excerpt from her address to policy makers about the need for reform.

> Injustice is also done to the convicts; it is certainly very wrong that they should be doomed day after day and night to listen to the ravings of madmen and madwomen. This is a kind of punishment that is not recognized by our statutes, and is what the criminal ought not to be called upon to undergo. The confinement of the criminal and of the insane in the same building is subversive of that good order and discipline which should be observed in every well-regulated prison. I do most sincerely hope that more permanent provision will be made for the pauper insane by the State, either to restore Worcester Insane Asylum to what it was originally designed to be or else make some just appropriation for the benefit of this very unfortunate class of our 'fellow-beings.'

Thinking Historically

1. Analyze Dorothea Dix's argument. Do you agree or disagree with her argument? Why?
2. Why were inmates and the insane housed together?
3. In her appeal, Dix referred to her appeal as a "sacred cause." Why?
4. Why is she viewed as a major reformer of the antebellum (before the Civil War) years?
5. Do you believe the legislators were receptive to Dix's appeal?

9

ADDICTION

One of the themes of American history is human rights and the question of how we have treated groups such as Native Americans, Africans, and, as we saw in the previous chapter, the people annexed by our war with Mexico. This theme deals with dignity and freedom. Since John Rolfe witnessed the arrival of the first Africans at Jamestown in 1619, we have been sensitive to how slavery and human bondage permeate our nation's past. The southern agricultural economy was dependent on human labor in the rice paddies, tobacco fields, and the Cotton Kingdom. Tensions erupted from time to time, bursting into insurrections like the 1739 Stono Rebellion.

The Founding Fathers argued about slavery, inserting a provision into the Constitution that, after 1808, slave importation would cease. The unfortunate reality, however, is that the slave population skyrocketed through breeding, and conditions of cruelty existed throughout the south. It became an addiction. Congress sought compromises, such as the 1820 Missouri Compromise, which admitted Missouri to the Union as a slave state and Maine as a free territory. Publications like David Walker's "The Appeal" and William Lloyd Garrison's *The Liberator* revealed the injustice of what came to be known as "the peculiar institution" of slavery, a system which most of the world's nations rejected.

The success in the Mexican War created an explosive situation as abolitionists who wished emancipation for enslaved people argued with pro-slavery leaders who wished to escape criticism of "the peculiar institution." Victory in the war did, indeed, "poison" us: Could the annexed land be fertile for cotton production? Would more slave states upend the balance between free and slave states in the Congress? How could peace be preserved in the Union?

In the aftermath of the war with Mexico, the presidents were weak: Polk was succeeded by Zachary Taylor who died in office in 1850 and was then succeeded by Millard Filmore who was followed in 1853 by Franklin Pierce. Weakness and instability in the executive branch. In Congress, however, there was towering strength. Three senators, hailing from different regions but sharing a belief that a solution could dilute the "poison" created by the acquisition of new territory, stepped forward to prevent a war over slave expansion in the territories. South Carolina's John C. Calhoun, Kentucky's Henry Clay, and Massachusetts's Daniel Webster drafted the Compromise of 1850.

California, where gold had been discovered the previous year, would enter the Union without slavery. Texas's debt would be paid by the federal government, and slavery would continue there. In the southwest, voters would settle the issue through "popular sovereignty," a referendum on slave versus free soil. Slave markets in Washington, DC, where the pain of human bondage could be witnessed and heard daily, were closed. Importantly, runaway slaves, fleeing with the help of sympathetic abolitionists, would be apprehended by the federal government and returned to their owners under the Compromise's Fugitive Slave Provision. Unfortunately, the agreement only put off the national day of reckoning over our "addiction."

In 1852, Harriet Beecher Stowe, a member of a prominent northern abolitionist family, published her novel *Uncle Tom's Cabin*, a searing indictment of the abuses and cruelty of slavery. Southern slave owners howled in criticism of what they considered Stowe's bias. After all, she had never visited the Deep South, only the border state of Kentucky, where slavery was permitted. Two years later, as the population of the Kansas Territory increased, Congress passed the Kansas-Nebraska Act, calling for popular sovereignty in the growing territory. The referendum turned into a mini-Civil War, "Bleeding Kansas," with bloodshed between pro- and anti-slave elements. Popular sovereignty proved to be chaotic. One incident was led by abolitionist John Brown in 1855 who murdered settlers that he deemed wrongly to be slavery supporters. Then, with the assistance of fellow abolitionists, Brown went into hiding.

A new political party, the Republican Party, had been formed in 1854. Its purpose was the end of slavery, even though Republicans disagreed over the means and time frame for such change. In 1856, this new political party nominated its first presidential candidate, Mexican War general John C. Fremont. The Democrats were victorious with Pennsylvania's James Buchanan, who had an impressive political resume but waffled on the slave question. It was hoped that Buchanan could navigate his party and the divided nation through the accelerating slavery debate, which erupted on the floor of the US Senate in 1856 with a pro-slavery House member, Preston Brooks, nearly beating to death Massachusetts's senator Charles Sumner—a beating that brought glee to white southerners and outrage to northerners.

Abolitionists led fugitive slaves northward on an Underground Railroad, in violation of the 1850 Fugitive Slave Provision, which the deceased Calhoun, Clay, and Webster had included in their compromise. And, just as Buchanan took office in 1857, the Supreme Court issued its *Dred Scott v. Sandford* decision in which Chief Justice Roger Taney, a Maryland slave owner, reminded the country that Scott, the property of a military doctor, was destined for permanent bondage despite the fact that the physician had been stationed on free soil at times. The ruling was clear: once a slave, always a slave. Southerners considered the ruling a victory; abolitionists believed it was outrageous.

By 1859, it was clear that America had been poisoned by Texas, just as the poet observed. The South's addiction to its "peculiar institution," quarrels over popular sovereignty, fugitive slaves, the *Dred Scott* decision, lack of civility, and poor national leadership were further aggravated by the return of John Brown, who that year resurfaced at an arsenal at Harpers Ferry, Virginia. His band, supported by northern abolitionists, overpowered the guards and tried unsuccessfully to spark a massive slave rebellion across the South. Captured by Marines under the command of Colonel Robert E. Lee, Brown was hanged in December 1859. His unsuccessful raid made him a martyr to abolitionists and a demon to slave owners, further fraying relations between the sections as a presidential election year dawned.

Document 9.1. Calhoun's 1850 Swan Song

The Compromise of 1850 prevented the Civil War from erupting over the slave question. It admitted California to the Union as free soil, outlawed slave markets in the nation's capital, assumed the debt of Texas, authorized popular sovereignty in the southwest, and committed the federal government to prevent fugitive slaves from reaching freedom in the north. The Great Triumvirate of John C. Calhoun, Henry Clay, and Daniel Webster placed their considerable prestige behind the compromise. Near death with tuberculosis, South Carolina's Calhoun, who had served as vice president to two presidents and had been on the national stage since his war hawk days, had a senate colleague read the following statement on his behalf during the debate.

> How can the Union be saved? ... —by adopting such measures as will satisfy the States belonging to the Southern section, that they can remain in the Union consistently with their honor and safety. There is, again, only one way by which this can be effected, and that is—by removing the causes by which this belief had been produced. Do this, and discontent will cease—harmony and kind feelings between the sections restored—and every apprehension of danger to the Union removed.

Thinking Historically

1. Calhoun argued that the national government must be committed to the return of runaway slaves. What point did he miss?
2. Does he blame the abolitionists for encouraging slaves to flee northward?
3. Why did Clay and Webster support the Fugitive Slave Provision of the compromise?
4. All three national leaders would be deceased by 1852. How did their absence propel America toward Civil War?
5. How would you have responded to Calhoun's swan song?

Document 9.2. *Uncle Tom's Cabin*

Novels are fiction, but Harriet Beecher Stowe's 1852 book *Uncle Tom's Cabin* was a powerful indictment of the abuses of "the peculiar institution," selling one million copies within a year. A member of a New England abolitionist family, Stowe had not traveled to the Deep South, but her characters seemed real, and their interactions were poignant. She had witnessed fleeing slaves make their way through Ohio on the Underground Railroad. This is an exchange between Simon Legree and the slave Tom.

> "And now," said Legree, "come here, you Tom. You see, I telled ye I didn't buy ye jest for the common work. I mean to promote ye, and make a driver of ye; and tonight I ye may jest as well begin to get yer hand in. Now, ye jest take this yer gal and flog her; ye've seen enough of it to know how."
>
> "I beg Mas'r's pardon," said Tom, "hopes Mas'r won't set me at that. It's what I an't used to—never did—and can't do, no way possible."
>
> "Ye'll larn a pretty smart chance of things ye never did know, before I've done with ye!" said Legree, taking up a cowhide and striking Tom a heavy blow across the cheek, and following up the infliction by a shower of blows.

Thinking Historically

1. How close to the truth was Stowe's novel?
2. Did the fact that she had never visited the Deep South undermine Stowe's criticism of slavery's brutality?
3. Did her membership in the abolitionist Beecher family strengthen or weaken the scenes she depicted in *Uncle Tom's Cabin*?
4. Why had the slave owners of the South become so defensive of criticism by 1852?
5. How do you assess the popularity of this novel further divides the country?

Document 9.3. John Brown's Last Words

Slave insurrections struck fear into the white population of the South, most of whom owned no slaves. Since the 1739 Stono Rebellion, such insurrections were a threat to the social, political, and economic order of the agricultural section. John Brown, who had killed innocent people during the 1855 "Bleeding Kansas" bloodshed, launched an unsuccessful attack on Harpers Ferry's arsenal in 1859, an attack supported by Brown's abolitionist backers and designed to acquire weapons. Arrested and quickly sentenced to death, Brown addressed the public shortly before he was hanged that December.

> This court acknowledges, as I suppose, the validity of the law of God. I see a book kissed here which I suppose to be the Bible, or at least the New Testament. That teaches me that all things whatsoever I would that men should do to me, I should do even so to them. It teaches me, further, to "remember them that are in bonds, as bound with them." I endeavored to act up to that instruction. I say, I am yet too young to understand that God is a respecter of persons. I believe that to have interfered as I have done—as I have always freely admitted I have done—in behalf of His despised poor, was not wrong, but right.

Thinking Historically

1. What, exactly, was John Brown's defense for his raid on the arsenal?
2. Based on the provided source material, what was John Brown's goal?
3. Why did slave insurrections such as the one at Harpers Ferry worry southern whites?
4. Were the authorities trying to make an example of Brown to prevent further attempts to arm slaves?
5. Why did Brown become a martyr to those opposed to slavery?

10

WAR

Wars, like revolutions, do not just erupt; hostilities, differences, and grievances fester for years. In our nation's history, sectional differences between North and South had been evident for centuries. Economic conflict was evident over issues such as the Bank of the United States, tariffs, and industrialization. At the heart of our Civil War, however, the root cause was slavery, the South's reliance on forced labor by Africans, and the abolitionists' increasing abhorrence of a cruel system that most of the world had abandoned. As historian Kenneth Stampp's study of slavery in America makes clear, it was a "peculiar institution," divisive, cruel, and emotional.

The events of the 1850s discussed in the previous chapter make it clear that the United States was heading toward conflict. By the 1860 presidential election, the Democratic Party was split over the issue of expansion of slavery and a belief in the South that the federal government was not enforcing the 1850 Fugitive Slave Provision, part of that year's compromise. The new Republican Party was opposed to expansion, with many people favoring slave emancipation. Fringe political parties were formed, exacerbating the friction. With the country divided in 1860, Illinois's Abraham Lincoln, the Republican nominee, won.

Lincoln tried in his March 1861 inaugural address to be conciliatory toward the South, but the previous month, with James Buchanan still in office, the Confederate States of America had been created with Mississippi's Jefferson Davis as its president. A loose "confederacy," the 11 southern states that ultimately formed it, had been born to protect "the peculiar institution."

In April, Confederates fired on the federal installation of Fort Sumter, off the coast of South Carolina. Lincoln called for volunteers to defend the Union, and war arrived. Initially, Lincoln's goal was to restore the Union, but by the summer of 1861, it became obvious that sectional animosity was leading to a long war which would eventually result in 750,000 American combat deaths. At the First Battle of Bull Run (Manassas) in July, Union soldiers threw their weapons down and fled in retreat from that Virginia battlefield.

Throughout the remainder of 1861, Lincoln searched for generals who could use superior northern resources (population, money, transportation, supplies) to achieve victory over the South, which had capable commanders like Robert E. Lee and Thomas J. "Stonewall" Jackson, who had earned his heroic nickname at Bull Run. The South, lacking foreign assistance and dwindling supplies, won key battles in 1862 at a return engagement at Bull Run and Fredericksburg, but by late that year, Lincoln changed justification for the war to the eradication of slavery—not merely preserving the Union (see Document 1.1). Additionally, he had successfully blockaded the South's coast and managed to hold on to the Border States, where, interestingly, slavery existed. As Document 1.1 makes clear, Lincoln's Emancipation Proclamation liberated the slaves in the rebelling states. This action crippled the South's agricultural economy as slaves headed northward, enlisting in President Lincoln's army. The Civil War had become a moral crusade, and "the peculiar institution" had few friends.

The year 1863 saw the Confederates triumph at Chancellorsville, but General Jackson was accidentally mortally wounded by his own men. And, by July, the South was split at Vicksburg along the strategic Mississippi River. Lincoln's efforts to find able commanders, such as General Ulysses S. Grant, were bringing success. Simultaneously, Lee gambled on an invasion of the North, but the Battle of Gettysburg was a crushing defeat for the Confederacy.

The Union duo of Grant and General William T. Sherman used their advantages to drain the enemy. Grant defeated Lee at the Wilderness in 1864, and Sherman marched through the southland, laying waste to the fields and terrorizing the civilians as he practiced "total war." Atlanta was burned, and Lincoln secured re-election as the year ended.

The reelected Lincoln, defeating one of his former generals, Democrat George McClellan, who advocated peace between the North and South, for the presidency, chose Andrew Johnson, a pro-Union Tennessean, as his running mate. Reconciliation was on Lincoln's mind as he called for healing the nation's wounds. On the battlefields, Grant pursued Lee's ill-equipped army into Virginia, and Sherman ravaged South Carolina, which saw its capital city of Columbia engulfed in flames. Grant encircled Lee outside of Richmond in April 1865, and Sherman advanced into North Carolina. Assessing the dire military situation, Lee surrendered to Grant at Appomattox Court House. Lincoln and First Lady Mary Todd Lincoln celebrated the victory by attending an April 12, 1865, performance of *Our American Cousin* at Washington's Ford's Theater, where Confederate sympathizer and actor John Wilkes Booth waited with a pistol, claiming through Lincoln's tragic assassination another casualty of the Civil War.

Document 10.1. A Divided Union, 1860

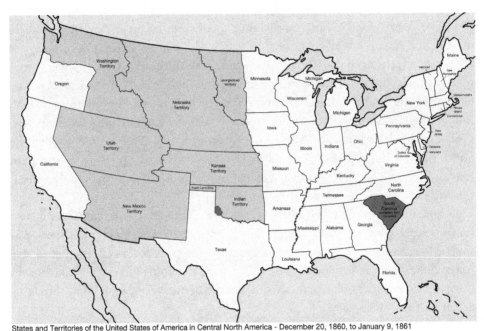

States and Territories of the United States of America in Central North America - December 20, 1860, to January 9, 1861

Fig. 10.1: Copyright © by Golbez (CC BY-SA 4.0) at https://en.wikipedia.org/wiki/File:United_States_Central_map_1860-12-20_to_1861-01-09.png.

This map illustrates the United States on the eve of the Civil War. Eleven southern states led by South Carolina, the Cotton Kingdom, formed the Confederate States of America. The slaveholding border states of Kentucky, Maryland, Delaware, and Missouri remained loyal to Lincoln, part of his strategy.

Thinking Historically

1. What advantages did the North have on the eve of the Civil War?
2. Why would a lengthy conflict favor the North?
3. Why was Lincoln's success in holding on to the border states crucial?
4. Discuss the strategic role played by the Mississippi River and the southern coastal cities.
5. Why, in your judgment, did the South embark on a doomed military effort?

Document 10.2. South Carolina Leaves the Union, 1860

South Carolina's differences with the federal government went back decades. The Nullification Crisis, fleeing slaves, and the flawed Compromise of 1850 document the state's hostility toward the nation's policy makers. By late 1860, with Abraham Lincoln elected president, South Carolina opted to secede. The following is an excerpt from the state's December 1860 Ordinance of Secession.

An ordinance to dissolve the Union between the State of South Carolina and other States united with her under the compact entitled "The Constitution of the United States of America." ...

On the 4th of March next (1861), this party (Republicans) will take possession of the government. It has announced that the south (and slaves) shall be excluded from the common territory; that the judicial tribunals shall be made sectional, and that a war must be waged against slavery until it shall cease throughout the United States.

Thinking Historically

1. Why did South Carolina consider it a constitutional right to leave the Union?
2. Why did the electoral success of the Republican Party disturb South Carolina?
3. Did the fact that 43 percent of white South Carolinians owned slaves lead to secession, a far bigger number than other southern states?
4. Did secession have a valid constitutional rationale?
5. In your opinion, did South Carolina expect that this document would prevent bloodshed?

Document 10.3. President Lincoln's View, 1861

Four presidential candidates vied for the White House in the 1860 election. One was pro-South, one favored "popular sovereignty" in the territories, one favored "the Constitution" and "the Union," and the other was Abraham Lincoln, the standard-bearer of the anti-slavery Republican Party. While Lincoln said slavery made him "miserable," he attempted to comfort the South in his March 1861 inaugural address, excerpted as follows:

> I am loath to close. We are not enemies, but friends. We must not be enemies. Though passion may have strained it must not break our bonds of affection. The mystic chords of memory, stretching from every battlefield and patriot grave to every living heart and hearthstone all over this broad land, will yet swell the chorus of the Union, when again touched, as surely they will be, by the better angels of our nature.

Thinking Historically

1. Even in the heated climate of the postelection, why was the new president attempting to reach out to the South?
2. Could a satisfactory solution other than a bloody Civil War have occurred?
3. What political realities did Lincoln face in the spring of 1861?
4. Why did the Confederacy respond the following month with the bombardment of Fort Sumter?
5. Was there no chance of reconciliation between the sections after Lincoln assumed the presidency?

Document 10.4. Mary Boykin Chesnut's Diary

The daughter of a former South Carolina governor and the wife of a former US senator who had resigned his seat in that body to serve the Confederacy, Mary Boykin Chesnut had a front-row seat to observe much of the Civil War, from the fall of Fort Sumter to the disintegration of her beloved South, of which she was a member of the ruling elite. Along the way, while her husband was off fighting, Chesnut kept a diary. The following are a few excerpts from her massive *Diary from Dixie*.

> We are busy looking after poor soldiers' wives. (I mean the wives of poor soldiers.) There is no end of them, and they never have less than nine or ten children. They are borrowing for the unreturning brave, hoping they will return and support their large families once more.
>
> The whole duty here consists in abusing Lincoln and the Yankees, praising Jeff Davis and the army of Virginia, and wondering when this horrid war will be over.
>
> They say all Yankees are splay-footed. As they steadily tramp this way, I must say I have ceased to admire their feet myself. How beautiful are the feet, etc. says the Scripture.
>
> Eat, drink, and be merry; tomorrow ye die. They say that, too.

Thinking Historically

1. How does Mary Chesnut's diary help us understand the human cost of the war to the South?
2. As a member of the slaveholding southern elite, is there something missing from Chesnut's *Diary from Dixie*?
3. How has a prolonged war affected Chesnut's life?
4. Why is a primary source such as this valuable for us?
5. Why does she, in her diary, see a societal kinship between women and slaves?

Document 10.5. Lincoln's Gettysburg Address

General Lee's 1863 gamble of invading the north failed with a three-day battle at Gettysburg, Pennsylvania in the summer. Later that year, President Lincoln came to the site to dedicate a cemetery holding the remains of the fallen warriors. By this point in the Civil War, the tide was turning against the South, even though the conflict would continue until the spring of 1865. Following is an excerpt from the president's Gettysburg Address.

> The world will little note nor long remember what we say here, but it can never forget what they did here. It is for us, the living, rather, to be dedicated here to the unfinished work which they who fought here have so far nobly advanced. It is rather for us to be here dedicated to the great task remaining

before us—that from these honored dead we take increased devotion to that cause for which they gave the last full measure of devotion; that we here highly resolve that these honored dead shall not have died in vain; that this nation, under God, shall have a new birth of freedom; and that government of the people, by the people, for the people, shall not perish from the earth.

Thinking Historically

1. How does Lincoln's Gettysburg Address show us his ultimate goal?
2. Why is this speech considered one of the president's most memorable addresses?
3. Why do historians rate Lincoln as our most successful president?
4. How has Lincoln's justification for the war changed since the conflict began?
5. Is there any doubt in your mind that the president will complete the war, regardless of how long it takes?

FAILURE

R ace and ethnicity in America have been themes that have flowed through our history since Christopher Columbus encountered indigenous people on the Caribbean's beaches in 1492. Cultures have interacted, and it has not always been as equal partners. Andrew Jackson's Indian removal policies of the 1830s shoved the natives westward, far from their ancestral homelands. A questionable war with Mexico from 1846 through 1848 is further evidence of an America where people of color were considered inferior.

Perhaps the clearest example of racism in our past has been the treatment of African Americans, those people who Virginia's John Rolfe witnessed arriving in Jamestown in 1619. Quickly, these individuals became permanent laborers in the tobacco fields of the Chesapeake and the rice paddies of South Carolina. Ships arrived with human cargo, and Africans were sold in the slave markets of America. Rebellions by people who wished to be free occurred, and tension arose in the South between whites and blacks.

The Founding Fathers, all white men, designated slaves three-fifths of a person in our 1787 Constitution. While importation of slaves was prohibited after 1808 by that document, "the peculiar institution" flourished with breeding. The Compromise of 1850 required the federal government to support the return of fugitive slaves, essential "property" for the cotton growers of the South. Abolitionists, outraged, grew in number as they read about abuses, such as those depicted in William Lloyd Garrison's *The Liberator* and Harriet Beecher Stowe's *Uncle Tom's Cabin*.

In 1857, the United States Supreme Court reminded everyone of the racial color line in America in the ruling of *Dred Scott v. Sandford*. Once a slave, always a slave. Southern states had enacted measures to prevent the education of blacks in an attempt to keep them docile and ignorant, treating them almost like dependent children.

As we saw in the last two chapters, the pathway to the Civil War was clearly defined by a sectional divide over the slave question. While President Lincoln initially wanted to reunite the country, he shifted his rationale for the war, which cost 750,000 American lives to a battle for freedom. Ironically, "freedom" has been another historical theme for us. From 1861 through 1865, it became a powerful force, with Lincoln emancipating the slaves in the rebelling states in early 1863. His plans for preparing slaves for a new life, however, were cut short by the events in Ford's Theater on the evening of April 12, 1865.

Abraham Lincoln's assassination elevated Andrew Johnson to the presidency. Coming from humble origins, Johnson had remained loyal to the Union when Tennessee seceded in 1861. Lincoln placed the southerner on the ticket as his vice-presidential running mate in 1864 as a gesture to the South, never expecting him to ever become president. John Wilkes Booth changed this plan at Ford's Theater, and a man of limited capabilities now directed the rebuilding, the reconstruction of our nation.

Johnson sought to emulate Lincoln; his plan for healing the nation's wounds, Presidential Reconstruction, was lenient. Southern leaders had to request pardons and adhere to the Constitution's Thirteenth Amendment which formally ended slavery. The new president sent Carl Schurz as an emissary to the South to report on the reconciliation that Johnson believed was taking place. Congress was not in session in 1865, so Johnson moved along with quick actions even when newly formed groups like the Ku Klux Klan terrorized the ex-slaves, freedmen, and freedwomen. To Johnson, ending slavery was all that was necessary; rebuilding the shattered South, changing racial attitudes, and addressing the needs of 4,000,000 freedmen and freedwomen were not needed.

When Congress returned to Washington in 1866, Radical Republicans were outraged by Johnson's leniency toward the South. This group was led by Charles Sumner, who had been beaten on the Senate floor in 1856 by Representative Preston Brooks, and Thaddeus Stevens, who had progressive views on race. The South was divided into military districts with Union troops, some ex-slaves, patrolling the countryside. Former Confederates were prevented from serving in high offices. Congressional Reconstruction, which took form in 1866, was based on the assumption that the freedman and freedwomen deserved assistance and protection. Changing white attitudes, the congressional leaders believed, would take considerable time.

Johnson, who lacked Lincoln's political and oratorical skills, saw things differently as he wrestled with the assertive Congress. The president vetoed the Civil Rights Bill and the Freedmen's Bureau Bill, both of which promoted extensive aid and protection to the former slaves. Both measures were passed by overriding the president's veto. Johnson aggravated the relationship with Congress by campaigning against his opponents in the 1866 midterm elections, all of whom won reelection.

By 1867, Congressional Reconstruction had eclipsed Johnson's approach. The Freedmen's Bureau became an extensive economic and educational network throughout the South. Congress drafted another amendment to the Constitution, ratified in 1868, guaranteeing equal protection and due process for the ex-slaves. The president considered the Fourteenth Amendment unnecessary. Additionally, Congress passed the Command of the Army Act, over Johnson's veto, giving military command to General Ulysses Grant instead of the president, who considered himself commander in chief.

Similarly, the 1867 Tenure of Office Act restricted Johnson's ability to remove cabinet secretaries, such as Secretary of War Edwin M. Stanton, who had allied himself with Congress, without that body's approval. The battle between Johnson and Congress, a constitutional crisis, climaxed with the president's 1868 impeachment. In a Senate vote,

Johnson was saved by a margin of one vote, in effect becoming politically impotent for the remainder of his term.

In the 1868 presidential election, Grant triumphed, but he brought with him to Washington unscrupulous individuals, many of whom were former military aides to the former general who made money off Reconstruction, as well as railroad construction. This corruption, although it did not involve Grant personally, came to be known as "Grantism." The president's commitment to the former slaves led to the 1871 Ku Klux Klan Trials, legal hearings designed to thwart the terrorists who roamed the countryside.

Throughout his two terms in the White House, Grant tried to protect African Americans with limited success while building railroads and supporting northern industrialization. The South continued to be devastated from the recent war, and the Klan continued its terrorist activities. At night, these white supremacists intimidated freedmen and freedwomen and interfered with the 1870 Fifteenth Amendment, which gave African American males the right to vote.

By 1876, "Grantism" and the lack of success in rebuilding the country, as well as failing to change racial views, set the stage for a key presidential election. Democrats chose the governor of New York, Samuel J. Tilden, and Republicans nominated Ohio governor Rutherford B. Hayes. Neither candidate won a sufficient number of Electoral College votes despite Tilden's 250,000 popular vote majority. Disputed returns in southern states, Florida, Louisiana, and South Carolina, led to a commission to investigate intimidation of Black voters and other irregularities. Meeting at Washington's Wormley House, commission members were courted and bribed by both political parties. Finally, in 1877, a compromise was reached: 20 disputed electoral votes were awarded to Hayes, giving him victory by the slimmest margin. He agreed to appoint a white southerner to a top government position, make significant funds available to rebuild the South's shattered infrastructure, and remove Union troops from the former Confederacy, thus abandoning the ex-slaves.

Reconstruction ended with a thud, a 12-year-long failure. Johnson had quarreled with Congress over the pace and direction of assisting African Americans. Grant, committed to them, had been hampered by his crooked cronies. And Hayes had become president under questionable circumstances. The plight of freedmen and freedwomen was ignored as our government focused its attention on economic growth and industrialization. Racial justice, a time-consuming and costly process, was no longer a goal as 1877 began, and captains of industry, bold entrepreneurs like John D. Rockefeller, Andrew Carnegie, and J. P. Morgan dominated America.

The failure of Reconstruction ends this anthology. By 1877, the country's attention turned to what writer Mark Twain called "the Gilded Age," a time (1877–1901) when wealth such as that on display at the Vanderbilt family's North Carolina palatial estate of Biltmore, a "hunting lodge" to that influential family, dominated headlines. Rockefeller's Standard Oil monopolized the oil industry. Carnegie, a Scottish immigrant, created U.S. Steel, America's first $1,000,000,000 industry, producing steel to construct cities with the hard labor of new immigrants from Eastern Europe. Morgan and his financial gigantic mega-bank, the House of Morgan, financed the growth.

Inventions like Alexander Graham Bell's telephone came to outnumber indoor toilets by 1900 as Americans communicated with each other during the Gilded Age. Rochester, New York's, George Eastman provided KODAK cameras to record the activities of a nation fascinated with itself. Lancaster, Pennsylvania's, Frank Woolworth sold an assortment of cheap goods in Woolworth Dime Stores in American cities. John Patterson, of Dayton, Ohio, developed a "thief catcher" used in small stores as a cash register to keep tabs on the sale of goods.

Left out of the thrilling progress were groups such as women, who did not get the right to vote until 1920. Farmers, realizing that agriculture with its dependency on weather and financing was not our nation's future, lost influence as wealth was measured in gold, much of it controlled by the House of Morgan. The indigenous people, those whose ancestors crossed Beringia 30,000 years earlier, had been resettled on reservations, which denied them citizenship in their own country. The new immigrants who comprised a new labor source found in the Gilded Age that the promise of America would be denied them in the steel mills, oil fields, and manufacturing plants. "The golden door" of the Statue of Liberty led too often to drudgery and low wages as the United States industrialized. The "huddled masses yearning to be free," as Emma Lazarus poignantly called them on that statue's inscription, came to America, as others had come, under duress and dreamed of a better life.

At the dawn of this Gilded Age, we find a nation controlled by those who had wealth and power, often more power than the president. With Rutherford Hayes and his successors beholden to the captains of industry, economic development and the creation of an empire that stretched to Asia took priority and left behind African Americans, abandoned by the deal that withdrew troops from the South and installed Hayes in the presidency in 1877. America entered what Professor Alain Locke called "the nadir of the Negro." Indeed, it was the low point for anyone wishing to continue racial healing.

Document 11.1. Carl Schurz Investigates Reconstruction, 1865

As this chapter explains, President Andrew Johnson, a white southerner who Lincoln put on the Republican Party ticket in 1864 as a gesture of reconciliation to the South, believed in a lenient restoration of the Union. With Congress in recess, Johnson sent a German American reformer to visit the defeated section in 1865 to document the contrition of the former rebels. Unfortunately, Schurz found little remorse or change in racial attitudes. He discovered them "not conquered but only overpowered." The following are Schurz's impressions of white Georgians in the aftermath of the war.

> They have a rope ready for this and that Union man when the Yankee bayonets are gone. They will show the Northern interlopers that have settled down here to live on their substance the way home. They will deal

largely in tar and feathers. They have been in the country and visited this and that place where a fine business is done in the way of killing Negroes. They will let the Negro know what freedom is, only that the Yankee soldiers be withdrawn.

Such is their talk. You can hear it every day, if you have your ears open. You see their sullen, frowning faces at every street corner.

Thinking Historically

1. Why did President Johnson send Schurz to the South so soon after the war's conclusion?
2. What did the president expect his emissary to find?
3. Do you believe Schurz's report to be accurate?
4. How did his visit undermine the premise of Presidential Reconstruction?
5. How did Congress react when it reconvened?

Document 11.2. Mary Ames's 1865 Letter to the President

Landownership and educational opportunities had been denied to slaves. Once the war was over, however, freedmen and freedwomen sought the government's support for guaranteeing property acquisition so that they could secure economic security. This October 1865 letter, compiled by New Englander Mary Ames on behalf of Blacks on South Carolina's Edisto Island, illustrates the fear that Reconstruction would not be simple.

> We the freedmen of this Island and the State of South Carolina—Do hereby petition to you as the President of these United States, that some provisions be made by which Every colored man can purchase land. And Hold it as his own. We wish to have A home if it be but A few acres. Without some provision is Made our future is sad to look upon. Yess our Situation is dangerous. We therefore look to you In this trying hour as A true friend of the poor and Neglected race, for protection and Equal Rights, with the purchase of A Homestead—A Homestead right here in the Heart of South Carolina.

Thinking Historically

1. Why were white southerners trying to deny former slaves landownership?
2. Why would the president be insensitive to pleas such as those found in Ms. Ames's letter?
3. What flaws do you detect in Johnson's approach to Reconstruction?
4. Would landownership help protect "equal rights" for freedmen?
5. How would Congress respond to Johnson's reluctance to protect the rights of southern blacks?

Document 11.3. The Ku Klux Klan's "Principles"

Organized in Pulaski, Tennessee, in 1865 as a Confederate veterans' association, the Ku Klux Klan (KKK) was quickly hijacked by white southerners intent on terrorizing freedmen and freedwomen. Using violence, the KKK attempted to resist Reconstruction and attempts at racial equality. While Union troops occupied the South as part of Congressional Reconstruction, the Klan was "an invisible empire," active in the dark as it roamed the countryside instilling fear in Blacks. The following is an 1868 statement of the organization's purposes.

> To protect the weak, the innocent, and the defenseless, from the indignities, wrongs, and outrages of the lawless, the violent, and the brutal; to relieve the injured and oppressed; to succor the suffering and unfortunate, and especially the widows and orphans of Confederate soldiers. ...
>
> To aid and assist in the execution of all constitutional laws, and to protect the people from unlawful seizure, and from trial except by their peers in conformity to the laws of the land.

Thinking Historically

1. Why did white southerners believe groups such as the KKK were necessary?
2. Why did these organizations flourish during Reconstruction?
3. What "defenseless" people are the Klan protecting?
4. What "constitutional laws" does the Klan endorse? Why?
5. Why is President Johnson unable to grasp the violence of the Klan?

Document 11.4. The Klan and Elias Hill, 1872

Unlike Johnson, President Ulysses Grant attempted to break the KKK's hold on the South. He worked with Congress to investigate the terrorist organization's use of violence and intimidation against Blacks by supporting early 1870s trials of suspected Klan members, all of whom denied under oath their membership. It was, indeed, an "invisible empire," the authorities discovered. The case of Elias Hill, a disabled Black South Carolinian, reveals the lawlessness of the Klan's "dens," as they were called. Hill testified before Congress in 1872, and the following is an excerpt of the Joint Committee on Reconstruction.

> After they had stayed in the house for a considerable time, they came back to where I lay and asked if I wasn't afraid at all. They pointed pistols at me all around my head once or twice, as if they were going to shoot me. ... One caught me by the leg and hurt me, for my leg for forty years has been drawn each year, more and more, and I made moan when it hurt so. One said, "G_d d___n it, hush!" He had a horsewhip, (and) I reckon he struck me eight cuts right on the hip bone; it was almost the only place he could

hit my body, my legs are so short. They all had disguises. ... One of them took a strap, and buckled it around my neck and said, "Let's take him to the river and drown him." ...

Then they said, "Look here! Will you put a card in the paper to renounce all republicanism? Will you quit preaching?" I told them I did not know. I said that to save my life. ... They said if I did not they would come back the next week and kill me.

Thinking Historically

1. Analyze the fear tactics that the Klan used against Elias Hill.
2. How did their use of "disguises" enable the Klan members to go undetected?
3. Compare Grant's approach to holding the Klan accountable with the approach of his predecessor.
4. Why, exactly, was the federal government unable to break the hold of "the invisible empire"?
5. Why did the presence of Union troops in the South during Reconstruction not deter the violence of the Klan?

Document Sources

T he 50 documents in this anthology permit us to hear the voices of history and its participants as we listen to the words of our past. Students are encouraged to read further, to research beyond these pages, pondering the events that shaped America from the people who walked across Beringia 30,000 years ago, to the indigenous men and women who greeted Christopher Columbus in 1492 on the Caribbean's beaches, to Puritan Anne Hutchinson who stood her ground as she spoke her mind in 1637, to the South Carolina slaves who tried to escape along the Stono River a century later, to the harsh sermons of Reverend Jonathan Edwards in 1741, to the colonists who asserted themselves against the mother country, to the plea of Abigail Adams in 1776 to "remember the ladies," to the soldiers who shivered at Valley Forge during the Revolution, to the Founding Fathers who framed a Constitution for posterity, to the Cherokees who resisted Indian removal in the 1830s, to the women of Seneca Falls, to the futile compromises as we headed toward Civil War, to the powerful words of *Uncle Tom's Cabin*, to the sounds of battle in the bloody conflict, to President Abraham Lincoln's inspiring call to the "better angels" of our nature, to the Ku Klux Klan that terrorized Elias Hill in 1872.

These are the sources for the documents found in this book:

Adams, Charles Francis. 1876. *Familiar Letters of John Adams and His Wife Abigail Adams*. Boston: Houghton Mifflin & Co.

"Address to the People of the United States, By South Carolina," *Washington National Intelligencer*, December 7, 1832.

American Colonies Act (6 George III c.12) 1766 Act of Parliament of Great Britain.

Ames, Mary. 1906. *From a New England Woman's Diary in Dixie in 1865*. Springfield, MA: Plimpton.

Anthony, Susan B., Elizabeth Cady Stanton, and Matilda Joslyn Gage, eds. 1889. *History of Woman Suffrage*. Rochester, NY: Charles Mann.

Arber, Edward, ed. 1910. *Travels and Works of Captain John Smith*. Edinburgh: John Grant.

Articles of Confederation, United States Congress, 1777.

Austin, Samuel, ed. 1808. *The Works of President Edwards*, Worcester: Isaiah Thomas.

Candler, Allen D., compiler. 1913. *The Colonial Records of the State of Georgia*, vol. 22, part 2, pp. 232–36. Atlanta: C.P. Byrd.

Chestnut, Mary Boykin. 1980. *A Diary from Dixie*. Edited by Ben Ames Williams. Cambridge: Harvard University Press.

Columbus, Christopher. 1492, October 11–12. *Journals*.

Congressional Globe. 1850. 31st Cong., 1st sess., 21, pt. 1, pp. 451–55.

Conway, Moncure Daniel, ed. 1894. *The Writings of Thomas Paine*. New York: Putnam.

Declaration of Independence. 1776, July 4.

Dorothea L. Dix. 1843. *Memorial to the Legislature on Massachusetts*. Boston: Munroe and Francis.

Eagles, Charles W., and Thomas S. Morgan, eds. 1988. "Abigail Adams to Mrs. W. S. Smith, November 21, 1800." In *Study Guide for Tindall's America: A Narrative History*, pp. 72–73. New York: W. W. Norton.

Escott, Paul D. 1983. *Slavery Remembered*. New York: Harper & Row.

Fitzpatrick, J. C., ed. 1938. *Writings of George Washington*. Washington, DC: U.S. Government Printing Office.

Government Printing Office. 1872. *Report of the Joint Select Committee to Inquire into the Condition of Affairs in the Late Insurectionary States*. Washington, DC: Government Printing Office.

Hutchinson, Thomas. 1936. *History of the Colony and Province of Massachusetts Bay*, vol. II, 1767. Cambridge: Harvard University Press.

Leininger, Phillip. 1995. *The Oxford Companion to American Literature*. Oxford: Oxford University Press.

Lester, J. C., and Wilson, D. C. 1905. *The Ku Klux Klan: Its Origins, Growth and Disbandment*. Edited by W. L. Fleming. New York: Neale.

Lincoln, Abraham 1897. "First Inaugural Address, March 4, 1861." In *Messages and Papers*, edited by James D. Richardson, vol. 6, p. 588. Washington: United States Government Printing Office.

Lincoln, Abraham. 1905. "Address at Gettysburg, Penn., November 19, 1863." In *The Writings of Abraham Lincoln*, Constitutional edition, edited by Arthur Brooks Lapsley, vol. 7, p. 20. New York and London: G.P. Putnam's Sons.

Lodge, H. C., ed. 1895. *The Federalist*. New York: G. P. Putnam's Sons.

Mahaffey, Joseph H., ed. "Carl Schurz's Letters from the South," *The Georgia Historical Quarterly*, vol. 35, no. 3 (September 1951), pp. 243–249.

Meyers, Albert Cook, ed. 1912. *Narratives of Early Pennsylvania, West Jersey, and Delaware*. New York: Charles Scribner's Sons.

Mittleberger, Gottlieb. 1898. *Journey to Pennsylvania in the Year 1750 and Return to Germany in the Year 1754*. Philadelphia: J. J. McVey.

Murray, John. 1776, November 7. Earl of Dunmore, Royal Governor of Virginia.

Nicolay, John, and John Hay, ed. 1905. *Complete Works of Abraham Lincoln*, vol. III. New York: Francis D. Tandy Company.

Parkman, Francis. 1896. *France and England in North America: Part Seventh*, Molcalm and Wolfe. Boston: Little, Brown and Co.

Polk, James K. "To the Senate and House of Representatives, May 11, 1846." In *A Compilation of the Messages and Papers of the Presidents 1789–1902*, vol. IV. Edited by James D. Richardson.

Poore, Benjamin P. ed. 1877. *The Federal and State Constitutions, Colonial Charters, and other Organic Laws of the United States*, vol 1. Washington, DC: Government Printing Office.

Portillo, Miguel Leon, ed. 1962. *The Broken Spears: The Aztec Account of the Conquest of Mexico*. Boston: Beacon Press.

Preston, Howard W., ed. 1886. *Documents of American History, 1606–1863*. New York: G. P. Putnam's Sons.

Quaritch, Bernard. 1893. *The Spanish Letter of Columbus to Luis de Sant Angel*. London: B. Quaritch.

Richardson, James D., ed. 1904. *A Compilation of the Messages and Papers of the Presidents 1789–1902*, vols. 1 & 11. Bureau of National Literature and Art.

Ruchames, Louis, ed. 1959. *A John Brown Reader*. London: Abeland-Schuman.

Stowe, Harriet B. 1852. *Uncle Tom's Cabin*. Boston: J. P. Jewett.

The Pennsylvania Gazette. 1812, March 11. "The Indian Prophet and His Doctrine."

The United States Constitution. 1789. "Amendment I."

The United States Constitution. 1789. "Preamble."

Tracy, E. C. 1845. *Memoir of the Life of Jeremiah Evarts*. Boston: Crocker and Brewster.

Waldo, Albigence. "Valley Forge, 1777–1778. Diary of Surgeon Albigence Waldo, of the Connecticut Line," *Pennsylvania Magazine of History and Biography*, vol. 21, no. 3 (1897), pp. 306–307.

About the Author

A former president of the South Carolina Historical Association, Dr. Edward Lee is a 36-year veteran of the university classroom, receiving several awards at Winthrop University, where he is a professor of history, for his teaching, including one 20 years ago as a pioneer in distance learning. He is the author of 16 books, which include three on America's Vietnam experience and one on the American Civil War. Frequently, he serves as a media commentator on a wide range of topics. His commentary has appeared on CNN, NBC News, and National Public Radio. For 18 years, Dr. Lee served as mayor of York, South Carolina. Governor Nikki Haley awarded him the State Historic Preservation Award in 2016 for his successful efforts to save the historic York County Courthouse. Currently, he serves as vice chair of the State Archives' Review Board for the National Register of Historic Places.